PROMISED LAND
DISCOVERY GUIDE

The Faith Lessons™ Series
with Ray Vander Laan

PROMISED LAND
DISCOVERY GUIDE

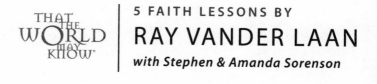

5 FAITH LESSONS BY
RAY VANDER LAAN
with Stephen & Amanda Sorenson

ZONDERVAN.com/
AUTHORTRACKER
follow your favorite authors

ZONDERVAN

Promised Land Small Group Edition Discovery Guide
Copyright © 1999, 2008 by Ray Vander Laan

Requests for information should be addressed to:
Zondervan, *Grand Rapids, Michigan 49530*

Focus on the Family and the accompanying logo and design are trademarks of
Focus on the Family, *Colorado Springs, Colorado 80995.*

That the World May Know and Faith Lessons are trademarks of Focus on the Family.

ISBN 978-0-310-27957-0

All maps are courtesy of International Mapping.

All artwork is courtesy of Ray Vander Laan unless otherwise indicated.

Interior design by Ben Fetterley

Printed in the United States of America

09 10 11 12 13 14 15 16 • 24 23 22 21 20 19 18 17 16 15 14 13 12 11 10 9 8 7 6 5 4 3 2

CONTENTS

INTRODUCTION

Because God speaks to us through the Scriptures, studying them is a rewarding experience. The inspired human authors of the Bible, as well as those to whom the words were originally given, were primarily Jews living in the ancient Near East. God's words and actions spoke to them with such power, clarity, and purpose that they wrote them down and carefully preserved them as an authoritative body of literature.

God's use of human servants in revealing himself resulted in writings that clearly bear the stamp of time and place. The message of the Scriptures is, of course, eternal and unchanging — but the circumstances and conditions of the people of the Bible are unique to their times. Consequently, we most clearly understand God's truth when we know the cultural context within which he spoke and acted and the perception of the people with whom he communicated.

This does not mean that God's revelation is unclear if we don't know the cultural context. Rather, by learning how to think and approach life as the people of the Bible did, modern Christians will deepen their appreciation and understanding of God's Word. Unfortunately, many Christians today do not have even a basic knowledge of the world and people of the Bible. This series is designed to help solve that problem. We will be studying the people and events of the Bible in their geographical, historical, and cultural contexts.

Although the DVD segments offer the latest archaeological research, this series is not intended to be a definitive historical, cultural, or geographical study of the lands and times of the Bible. No original scientific discoveries are revealed here. My goal is simply to help us better understand the message of the Bible. Once we know the *who, what,* and *where* of a Bible story, we will be able to better understand the *why*. By deepening our understanding of God's Word, we can more clearly see God's revealed mission for our lives and strengthen our relationship with him.

The Assumptions of Biblical Writers

For this study, it is important to realize that people today use the names *Israel* and *Palestine* to designate the land God gave to Abraham and that both terms are politically charged. *Palestine* is used by the Arabs living in the central part of the country, while *Israel* is used by the Jews to indicate the State of Israel. In this study, however, *Israel* is used in the biblical sense. This choice does not indicate a political statement regarding the current struggle in the Middle East, but is chosen because it best reflects the biblical designation for the land.

Biblical writers assumed that their readers were familiar with Near Eastern geography, history, and culture. They used a language which, like all languages, is bound by culture and time. For example, the people whom God chose as his instruments — the people to whom he revealed himself — lived in the Near East, where people typically described their world and themselves in concrete terms. Their language was one of pictures, metaphors, and examples rather than ideas, definitions, and abstractions.

This is why the Bible is filled with concrete images. While we might describe God as omniscient or omnipresent (knowing everything and present everywhere), the people of the Bible would have preferred to describe God by saying, "The Lord is my Shepherd," or "God is our Father, and we are his children," or "God is the Potter, and we are the clay." So to understand the Scriptures, we need to know more than what the words mean, we need to understand them from the perspective of the people who thought and spoke in terms of those images every day of their lives. We need to know what it meant for them to recognize Jesus as the Lamb killed on Passover, and to think of heaven in terms of an oasis in the desert and hell being like a city sewage dump.

The people of the Bible also had an Eastern mind-set rather than a Western mind-set. Eastern thought emphasizes the process of learning as much as or more than the result. Whereas Westerners tend to collect information to find the right answer, Hebrew thought stresses the process of discovery as well as the answer. So as you go through this study, use it as an opportunity to deepen your understanding of who God is and to grow in your relationship with him.

Understanding the World of the Hebrews

More than 3,800 years ago, God spoke to his servant Abraham: "Go, walk through the length and breadth of the land, for I am giving it to you" (Genesis 13:17). From the outset, God's choice of a Hebrew nomad to begin his plan of salvation (a plan that is still unfolding today) was linked to the selection of a specific land where his redemptive work would take place. The nature of God's covenant relationship with his people demanded a place where their faith could be exercised and displayed to all nations so that the world would know of *Yahweh,* the true and faithful God.

The Promised Land, then, was the arena in which God's people were to serve him faithfully as the world watched. So if we are to fully understand God's plan and purpose for his people, we must also understand the nature of the place he selected for them. After all, God showed the same care in preparing a land for his chosen people as he did in preparing a people to live in that land.

The land God chose for his people was on the crossroads of the world. A major trade route of the ancient world, the Via Maris, ran through the land, and more than a million people a year traveled that route. God intended for the Israelites to take control of the cities along this route and thereby exert influence on the nations around them. Through their righteous living, the Hebrews were to reveal the one true God, *Yahweh,* to the world. (They failed to accomplish this mission, however, because of their unfaithfulness.)

Western Christianity tends to spiritualize the concept of the Promised Land as it is presented in the Bible. Instead of seeing it as a crossroads from which to influence the world, modern Christians tend to view it as a distant, heavenly city, a glorious "Canaan" toward which we are traveling as we ignore the world around us. We focus more on the destination than the journey and, in a sense, view our earthly experience as simply preparation for an eternity in the "promised land." We have unconsciously separated our walk with

God from our responsibility to the world in which he has placed us, which distorts our perception of the mission God has set for us.

Many Christians today have forgotten that the mission of God's people has always been to live *so that the world would know that their God was the true God.* This was true when the Hebrews left Egypt and possessed the Promised Land. It was true during the years of the exile in Babylon. It was true during the time Jesus lived on earth after the Jews had returned to Israel. And it was true for the disciples of Jesus who followed him as their Rabbi and obeyed his command to go out into the world and make disciples.

The life of faith is not a vague, otherworldly experience. Rather, it is being faithful to God right now, in the place and time in which he has put us. This truth is emphasized by God's choice of Canaan, a crossroads of the ancient world, as the Promised Land in which the Israelites were to live. Our mission as Christians today is the same one God gave to the Israelites when they possessed the Promised Land, the same one Jesus gave to his disciples. We are to love the Lord our God with all our heart, with all our soul, and with all our might, and to love our neighbors as ourselves so that through us *the world may know that our God is the one true God.*

STANDING AT THE CROSSROADS

The people who lived in the land of Israel left behind an indelible record of their lives. An important part of that record lies in large mounds called *tels,* which are piles of debris from ancient cities that over the centuries were destroyed and rebuilt, one on top of another. As archaeologists excavate tels, they peel away preserved layers of history and bring to light evidence of the culture, architecture, art, diet, weapons, and even writings of the people who lived in those ancient cities. Their findings about the culture and people of ancient Israel stand as a testimony to the truth of the words we read in the Bible.

This video focuses on Tel Gezer, one of the greatest tels in Israel. To stand on this huge mound is to stand on the ruins of as many as five thousand years of human history! Today, Tel Gezer's location in a quiet, agricultural region gives little indication of its importance in history. But in ancient times, Gezer was a bustling crossroads.

Gezer could be described as a city "in between." To understand this, we need to zoom out and consider the geography of Gezer and the ancient world. To the west is the fertile, coastal plain that lies along the Mediterranean Sea. To the east are the foothills — the *Shephelah* — beyond which lie the mountains of Judea and, beyond them, the forbidding Arabian Desert. So Gezer lies "between" the desert and the sea.

If we zoom out farther, we see Egypt, a technologically advanced world power southwest of Gezer. Far to the east lies Mesopotamia, the home of civilizations the Bible refers to as Persia, Babylon, and Assyria. Gezer was one of three cities in the land of

Israel that were located on the *Via Maris,* the main coastal road that ran "between" the mighty empires of Egypt and Mesopotamia. The Via Maris bustled with activity as those powerful civilizations shared economic and cultural ties.

Gezer was also one of few points where an east-west road intersected the Via Maris. The road ran east from Gezer into the mountains of Judea to Jerusalem and on toward Jericho and the King's Highway, which was another trade route (more difficult to travel than the Via Maris) east of the Jordan River. So the people of Gezer literally lived at the crossroads of the ancient world!

This session reveals the connection between Gezer's strategic location and God's plan for Israel. Whoever controlled the city could, in effect, dominate trade on the Via Maris and greatly influence the people and cultures of the ancient world. So God placed the children of Israel in Canaan, and specifically in cities such as Gezer, where they could make a difference, where they could be a powerful, "flavoring" influence on the world. God wanted his people to live out his salvation in everyday life, to demonstrate morality, justice, and compassion in such a way that the whole world would see it and know that the God of Israel is the one true God.

But for the most part, Israel failed to wrest control of the land and cities of Canaan, including Gezer. They never exerted the powerful influence God desired them to have as his witnesses to the world. Instead, they allowed the pagan culture of the Canaanites to flourish and exert its influence.

This insight into ancient history has a significant application for Christians today. God calls his people to stand at the crossroads and to actively participate in shaping our culture and our world. He calls us to be a flavoring influence on others and to live in such a way that when people see us, they also see God.

Opening Thoughts (4 minutes)

The Very Words of God

> The LORD had said to Abram, "Leave your country, your people and your father's household and go to the land I will show you.
>
> "I will make you into a great nation and I will bless you; I will make your name great ... and all peoples on earth will be blessed through you."
>
> *Genesis 12:1 – 3*

Think About It

God carefully chose a specific people, the descendants of Abraham, to become a nation and take part in unfolding his plan of salvation for the world. He also chose a specific place for those people to live and fulfill their role in bringing about his plan of salvation.

Today, God still chooses people to do the work of his kingdom on earth. Think for a moment about where you live, what you do, and the people with whom you have contact. Can you think of why God might have placed you where you are?

DVD Teaching Notes (22 minutes)

Tel Gezer: geographic and cultural crossroads

City gates: focal point of defense and administration

Israel: placed at the crossroads to accomplish God's plan

The message of standing stones

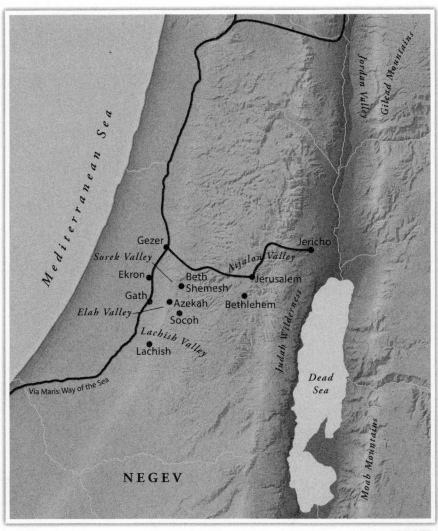

ISRAEL

DVD Discussion (6 minutes)

1. What was unique about Israel's location in the ancient world, and what made Tel Gezer particularly significant?

2. As inhabitants of the land of Israel, how much potential did God's chosen people have to demonstrate God's plan of salvation to their region and even the whole world?

    What did God require the Israelites to do in order to fulfill his plan, and what did they do that diminished their effectiveness?

3. In the cities of the ancient world, what purposes and activities were associated with city gates?

THE TRUTH OF THE MATTER

Even though the Israelites seldom inhabited Gezer, and thus allowed the Canaanites to wield much greater influence on the world's culture than they otherwise would have, the Canaanites living there did not have an easy life. In fact, the people of Gezer had a rough life. Consider:

- When Joshua led the Israelites into Canaan, Horam — the king of Gezer — attacked them, but Horam and his troops were all killed (Joshua 10:33).
- The tribe of Ephraim allowed the Canaanites to continue living in Gezer, but used them as forced labor (Joshua 16:10).
- Pharaoh, king of Egypt, attacked and captured Gezer and then set it on fire. He killed its Canaanite inhabitants and gave it as a wedding gift to his daughter, Solomon's wife (1 Kings 9:16).
- During King David's reign, the Israelites battled the Philistines at Gezer (1 Chronicles 20:4). Years later, Solomon rebuilt Gezer's walls (including its huge, six-chambered gate) using forced laborers (1 Kings 9:15–17).

Small Group Bible Discovery and Discussion (17 minutes)

God Chooses a People and a Place to Carry Out His Plan

For generations, God had prepared the Hebrews to be *his* people, to conquer the land of the Canaanites and make it the land of Israel, the nation of his chosen people. God clearly had designated a strategic region at the heart of the ancient world to be the land of Israel — a land with fertile soil and key trade routes — but why? Why did God choose these people and this particular place? What did he want his people to accomplish in the land he gave to them? Although these may seem like rhetorical questions to us, the Scriptures give us great insight into God's intentions.

1. Read Genesis 12:1 – 3 and 18:17 – 19.

    a.   Who did God choose to be the founder of Israel, and why did he choose this person?

    b.   What promise did God make concerning the nation of Israel?

    c.   What was God's purpose in establishing a nation for himself?

2.   How did God intend for the world to know who he was? (See Isaiah 43:1, 10 - 13.)

    In what ways could God's placement of his people in the land of Israel — at the crossroads of the ancient world — help accomplish this?

3.   What commitments did God make to his people before they entered Canaan? (See Exodus 6:6 - 8; 23:27 - 31; 34:10 - 11.)

    Why would these promises have been meaningful to God's chosen people as they went into Canaan?

    Why were these promises an important part of God's plan?

4. What do you think are the main reasons the Israelites failed to influence their culture and the world to the extent God intended?

5. Describe how you think God wants Christians today to live for him and use our position to exert influence in key areas of our culture so that "all the peoples of the earth may know that the LORD is God" (1 Kings 8:60).

   To what extent are the same reasons that limited the influence of the Israelites also limiting the influence of Christians today?

TEL GEZER

Faith Lesson (5 minutes)

God wants his people to greatly influence the culture of the world. That is why he placed his chosen people in the land of Israel and wanted them to occupy influential cities such as Gezer, where millions of people yearly passed through on the Via Maris. That is why Jesus said to his disciples, "You are the salt of the earth.... You are the light of the world.... let your light shine before men, that they may see your good deeds and praise your Father in heaven" (Matthew 5:13 – 16). And God still wants his followers today — you and me — to actively participate in and influence culture. He wants us to live so publicly that we "flavor" the culture of our world.

1. In what ways do you think God has placed you at an important "crossroads" in your world? And what are the specific arenas of life from which God wants you to show that he is the Lord God?

2. What do you do to publicly exert godly influence within your sphere of influence?

3. How does God's call for you to exhibit him in all that you do, think, and say affect what you do every day? In what ways does this call need to play a more prominent role in your life?

Closing (1 minute)

Read 1 Peter 2:9, 12 aloud: "You are a chosen people, a royal priesthood, a holy nation, a people belonging to God, that you may declare the praises of him who called you out of darkness into his wonderful light…. Live such good lives among the pagans that, though they accuse you of doing wrong, they may see your good deeds and glorify God on the day he visits us."

Then pray, asking God to use this session and the coming ones to give you a greater desire to love him and live for him with all your heart, soul, and strength. Ask him to increase your passion and commitment to influence your culture so that others will know that he is God.

Memorize

Live such good lives among the pagans that, though they accuse you of doing wrong, they may see your good deeds and glorify God on the day he visits us.

1 Peter 2:12

Making God Known to the World

In-Depth Personal Study Sessions

Day One | Living in Obedience to God's Plan

The Very Words of God

> *See, I am setting before you today a blessing and a curse — the blessing if you obey the commands of the LORD your God that I am giving you today; the curse if you disobey the commands of the LORD your God and turn from the way that I command you today by following other gods, which you have not known.*

> *Deuteronomy 11:26 – 28*

DID YOU KNOW?

The land God selected for his people was not like Mesopotamia or Egypt, where annual flooding of the Tigris and Euphrates rivers (Mesopotamia) and the Nile (Egypt) all but guaranteed fertile soil and adequate irrigation. Instead, God chose for his people a land where they would have to depend on rainfall, sent by God, for the survival of their crops and the feeding of their families. (See Deuteronomy 11:8 – 21.)

God promised blessing or judgment on the land dependent on the obedience of his people. If they obeyed, he would bless them by sending rain and abundant harvest. If they disobeyed, he would allow them to experience hardship by withholding the rain or allowing their enemies to harm them.

Bible Discovery

Obeying God Is Part of the Plan

God placed his people exactly where he wanted them to live and show the world the greatness of the God of Israel. Although God planned to bless his people in ways that would amaze the world, his people had to depend on him to provide for their needs and to obey him in all things. Their obedience was required for God's blessing to be fulfilled.

1. In what way(s) did God say the Promised Land would differ from the land of Egypt? (See Deuteronomy 11:8 – 12.)

2. What kind of life did God promise the Israelites if they faith-fully obeyed his commands? And what consequences did he promise if they chose to disobey and worship other gods? (See Deuteronomy 11:13 – 17, 22 – 25.)

3. How do we know that obedience to the Word and com-mands of God was of utmost importance, and how were the Israelites to keep God's Word? (See Deuteronomy 11:18 – 21.)

4. What do we know about the choices the Israelites made once they entered Canaan that altered God's plan for them? (See Joshua 13:13; 16:10; Judges 1:27 – 36.)

5. What were some of the consequences of Israel's failure to obey God? (See Judges 2:11 – 13, 19; 10:6 – 7; 1 Kings 14:22 – 24; 2 Kings 17:14 – 17; 21:9.)

Reflection

Take a few minutes to read Solomon's words to Israel following his prayers of dedication of the temple in Jerusalem (1 Kings 8:56 – 61) and consider how important the obedience of God's people is in fulfilling his plan of redemption for the world.

Why is it necessary for us, just as it was for the ancient Israelites, to demonstrate our trust in God through obedience?

What are some of the ways that we, living in a prosperous culture where self-sufficiency is the norm, need to obey God and depend on him?

What might be the consequences — to us and to our testimony to the world — when we fail to be the witnesses God has called us to be and don't develop an awareness of our dependence on God or choose not to obey his Word?

Day Two | Motivated to Stand at the Crossroads

The Very Words of God

"You come against me with sword and spear and javelin, but I come against you in the name of the LORD Almighty, the God of the armies of Israel, whom you have defied.... Today I will give the carcasses of the Philistine army to the birds of the air and the beasts of the earth, and the whole world will know that there is a God in Israel."

1 Samuel 17:45 – 46

Bible Discovery

Trusting God at the Crossroads

As a whole, the nation of Israel failed to live in obedience to God and, therefore, failed to display his greatness to the watching world. However, the Scriptures provide some remarkable examples of those who did recognize that they were standing "at the crossroads" and had a role to play in making the God of Israel known to the world.

1. Read 1 Samuel 17:1 - 11, 25 - 33, 36 - 37, 45 - 47.

    a. Who was the Philistine, Goliath, really challenging when he shouted against the armies of Israel? What was at stake? (See verses 8 - 10, 26.)

b.   What kinds of obstacles did David face as he sought to
     fulfill his role in making the God of Israel known to the
     world? (See verses 4 – 7, 28, 33.)

c.   Who did David recognize held the key to victory? (See
     verses 45 – 47.) Contrast his attitude and actions to those
     of the Israelite soldiers, to whom God had promised and
     demonstrated his power again and again.

2.   Years after he killed Goliath, when David was the new king
     of Israel, he faced another challenge from the Philistines.
     What was at stake this time, and what happened as a result
     of David's trust and obedience to God's commands? (See
     1 Chronicles 14:8 – 17.)

3.   Joshua, Elijah, and Hezekiah also faced challenges in the
     crossroads of life and chose to obey God in order to make
     him known. Read their stories and answer the related
     questions on page 26.

	What motivated his actions?	What risks did he face?	What resulted?
Joshua (Johua 4:19 – 24)			
Elijah (1 Kings 18:21 – 24, 36 – 40)			
Hezekiah (2 Kings 19:9 – 19)			

Reflection

Rahab, the prostitute in Jericho who protected the spies of Israel, told them, "We have heard how the LORD dried up the water of the Red Sea for you when you came out of Egypt, and what you did to Sihon and Og, the two kings of the Amorites east of the Jordan, whom you completely destroyed. When we heard of it, our hearts melted and everyone's courage failed because of you, for the LORD your God is God in heaven above and on the earth below" (Joshua 2:10 - 11).

In what ways do her words speak to you about the effectiveness of God's plan when his people stand at the crossroads and obey what he has called them to do?

In what ways do you think your position as a Christian in today's world is like Israel's position in the ancient world? How does your view affect your actions in daily life?

Think about when you have faced a difficult decision or challenge at a key crossroads in your life. In what ways did your response reveal God's greatness to the people of your world? In what ways did you fail to display God's greatness?

In a psalm recorded in 1 Chronicles 16:8 – 36, David expressed his commitment to honoring and trusting God so that the surrounding nations would see what God had done. How do you want the people who come after you to know the ways in which your life displayed God's greatness to your world? Take some time now to write your own psalm about your commitment to make God known in your world. Offer that psalm as a testimony to others and a prayer of thanksgiving to God for his great faithfulness, supreme majesty, and matchless glory.

Day Three | God Is Faithful to Carry Out His Plan

The Very Words of God

The plans of the LORD stand firm forever, the purposes of his heart through all generations.

Psalm 33:11

Bible Discovery

God Is Sovereign

The Bible, especially the Old Testament, teaches that God is "sovereign"—in absolute control of all things. He has the power and patience to carry out through human history everything he has planned and promised to do. Many times in history, God has demonstrated his power and faithfulness in fulfilling his plan of redemption by saving his chosen people from what appears to be certain destruction.

GOD IS FAITHFUL TO BRING ABOUT HIS PLAN OF REDEMPTION*

Date	Event
1875 BC	God establishes his covenant with Abraham
1670 BC	The sojourn to Egypt
1450 BC	Deliverance from Egypt to the Promised Land
1000 BC	David establishes peace; Solomon builds God's temple
900 BC	Kingdom divides
722 BC	Assyria destroys the Northern Kingdom (Israel)
586 BC	Fall of Jerusalem and exile of Judah to Babylon
500 BC	Return of the remnant to Jerusalem
AD 29	Death and resurrection of Jesus, the Messiah
???	The second coming of Jesus

* Most dates are approximate; exact dates unknown.

1. When a severe famine threatened the survival of Jacob's family—whose sons were to be the fathers of the twelve tribes of Israel—how did God save them? (See Genesis 41:25 - 32, 53 - 57; 42:1 - 5; 45:16 - 18; 46:5 - 7.)

   What role did standing at the crossroads and influencing the culture play in this story?

   What role did obedience to God play in this story?

2. What plot did Haman plan for the Jews, and how did God use Esther — the Jewish queen of the king of Persia — to save his people? (See Esther 2:8 - 10, 15 - 18; 3:1 - 6, 13 - 15; 4:1, 5 - 17; 5:1 - 8; 7:1 - 10.)

   What role did standing at the crossroads and influencing the culture play in this story?

What role did obedience to God play in this story?

3. At times, God's plans seem doomed to failure. One such instance occurred during King Hezekiah's reign when King Sennacherib of Assyria threatened to destroy Jerusalem. Read Isaiah 37:15 - 22, 26, 32 - 36. In light of God's plan to make himself known to the world, which significant truths are revealed in the following verses?

v. 16	
v. 17	
vv. 18 – 19	
v. 20	
v. 26	
vv. 32 – 34	
v. 35	

Reflection

Galatians 4:4 – 5 reveals a key truth about God's plan of redemption: "But when the time had fully come, God sent his Son, born of a woman, born under law, to redeem those under law, that we might receive the full rights of sons."

No matter how long it takes, no matter how great the challenges, God is faithful to bring about his salvation. But what about your faithfulness?

To what extent are you engaged at the crossroads and living to influence your culture for God?

To what extent have you abandoned your influence in certain aspects of culture?

What risks are you willing to take to trust God and sacrificially obey him so that his greatness will be revealed to a watching world?

What will be the consequences if you withdraw, isolate yourself, or ignore what God intends to accomplish at the crossroads of culture?

Memorize

But when the time had fully come, God sent his Son, born of a woman, born under law, to redeem those under the Law, that we might receive the full rights of sons.

Galatians 4:4–5

Day Four | City Gates

The Very Words of God

Dressed in their royal robes, the king of Israel and Jehoshaphat king of Judah were sitting on their thrones at the threshing floor by the entrance of the gate of Samaria, with all the prophets prophesying before them.

1 Kings 22:10

DID YOU KNOW?

SOLOMON'S GATE AT GEZER

During biblical times, city gates:

- Protected the entrance of the city from enemies.
- Functioned as the center of city life — like a city hall or courthouse today. In various chambers inside the gatehouse, people paid their taxes, set-

tled legal matters, and even met with the king. Soldiers were stationed there too.
- Provided a gathering place for prophets, kings, priests, judges, and other city leaders. For example, Jehoshaphat (king of Judah) and Ahab (king of Israel) sat on their thrones in the gate of Samaria (1 Kings 22:10).
- Created a natural place for merchants and vendors to conduct business because of the people coming and going through the gate.

Bible Discovery

To "Sit at the Gate"

The most significant remains of ancient cities found today are often the gateways. During biblical times, the city gate not only protected the city but also functioned as the administrative center or "city hall" and community center. Rulers, judges, and other officials "sat in the gate" to conduct the business of the city, and merchants gathered at the city gate to sell their goods.

What do the following Scripture passages reveal about the people and their function in relationship to the city gates?

Genesis 13:10 – 13; 18:20 – 21; 19:1 – 6, 9

Deuteronomy 21:18 – 21

Ruth 4:1 – 11

1 Samuel 4:10 – 18

2 Samuel 18:1 – 5; 19:1 – 8

Esther 2:5 – 8, 19 – 23

Reflection

Consider what the equivalent of the ancient city gates are in your world, and list the culture-influencing activities that take place there. To what extent are you involved in the activities of your "city gates"? In what ways might God want you to more actively participate in what takes place there and thereby have a greater influence on the culture of your world?

Begin praying about how God may want you to live for him and show his greatness in the city gates of your world.

THE ROLE OF THE EASTERN GATE IN THE LIFE OF THE MESSIAH

The Bible pictures the Messiah entering the temple through the Eastern (or Beautiful) Gate. Islamic leaders have taken this image so seriously that they have blocked the gate and built a cemetery in front of it in an attempt to prevent the Messiah (who would become ceremonially unclean if he touched anything connected with death) from entering the Temple Mount!

Not only will the Messiah enter the temple through the Eastern Gate, but tradition says that it will be the symbolic or literal location of the last judgment. Consider these Scriptures:

- *Joel 3:2, 12*—The last judgment will take place in the Jehoshaphat Valley, just east of Jerusalem.
- *Zechariah 14:1–11*—The power of God will establish Jerusalem as the heavenly city.
- *Isaiah 62:10; Revelation 21*—After the last judgment, the saved will enter the gate of the heavenly city. Since the setting is on the east side of Jerusalem, the gate will be the Beautiful or Eastern Gate.

Day Five | Standing Stones

The Very Words of God

> On that day Joshua made a covenant for the people, and there at Shechem he drew up for them decrees and laws. And Joshua recorded these things in the Book of the Law of God. Then he took a large stone and set it up there under the oak near the holy place of the LORD.
>
> **Joshua 24:25 – 26**

Bible Discovery

Becoming a Living, Standing Stone

God's work in the past — the distant past and our own — is the foundation on which our belief in God and commitment to him are built. Recognizing the importance of remembering what the one true God had done for them, his chosen people erected standing stones as memorials to his supernatural acts on their behalf, as did the Canaanites to their own gods centuries before the Israelites arrived.

1. What is the difference between the standing stone mentioned in Genesis 28:16 – 19 and those described in 1 Kings 14:22 – 23?

2. What do Exodus 23:24, Leviticus 26:1, and Deuteronomy 16:21 – 22 say about the pagan use of standing stones?

3. For each of the following passages, summarize the story or event and note the work of God that the standing stones commemorate or represent:

Genesis 35:1 – 3, 14 – 15

Exodus 24:1 – 5

Joshua 3:14 – 17; 4:4 – 9

Joshua 24:19 – 27

DID YOU KNOW?

At the high place at Gezer, ten stones (some more than twenty feet tall) stand in silent tribute to a now-forgotten event. Lonely sentinels on the ruins of ancient cities, such gigantic standing stones provide a glimpse into a custom popular thousands of years ago. Long before the Israelites entered Canaan, pagans in the ancient Near East erected sacred stones to their gods, to declare covenants and treaties between cities or individuals, and to honor gods they believed caused an important event or provided a significant benefit. The stones indicated to anyone who saw them that something significant had happened in that place.

The Hebrew word translated "standing stones" is *massebah* and means "to set up." Perhaps our practice of placing tombstones over the graves of loved ones is derived from a special standing stone called a *stele* (plural: *stelae*). In ancient times, these stones were erected as *masseboth* (standing stones) and had stories or inscriptions carved on them explaining their significance.

Archaeologists in the Middle East have unearthed many *stelae*, including one found in 1993 at Tel Dan that mentions the name "David"—the only extrabiblical reference to David ever discovered. To date, no *massebah* or *stele* specifically mentioned in the Bible has been found.

Reflection

Just as the people of ancient Israel erected "standing stones" to commemorate God's supernatural actions on their behalf, God wants each of us to be a *massebah* — a living, standing stone that God is shaping and cutting in order to build his kingdom. In the same way that people in ancient times were reminded of what God had done for them when they saw standing stones, God calls us to live godly lives so that the world will see our good deeds and want to know our God.

Who has been a standing stone for you? Who are the people who have influenced you and made you aware of God's work in their lives, thereby helping you to know and understand God?

What kind of standing stone are you? List the "monuments" in your life that proclaim to other people, "The Lord is God."

If the "monuments" of your life point more to your accomplishments than to God's greatness, what must you change?

Memorize

As you come to him, the living Stone — rejected by men but chosen by God and precious to him — you also, like living stones, are being built into a spiritual house to be a holy priesthood, offering spiritual sacrifices acceptable to God through Jesus Christ.... Live such good lives among the pagans that ... they may see your good deeds and glorify God.

1 Peter 2:4 – 5, 12

WET FEET

When you think of the Jordan River in Israel, what comes to mind? A wide, powerful river surging hundreds of miles toward the ocean? If so, you will be surprised when you see this video. In most places, the Jordan River is a mere fifty to seventy-five feet across! And as the crow flies, it is only ninety miles from where the springs of the Jordan begin flowing from the foot of Mount Hermon to the river's end at the Dead Sea.

Located at the northern end of the Great Rift Valley east of the mountains of Judea, the Jordan River is a prominent geographical feature in Israel. Mentioned 181 times in the Old Testament and eighteen times in the New Testament, the Jordan River played an important, but in some ways unusual, role in Israel's history. Many ancient peoples considered the key rivers of their homelands to be sacred (such as the Ganges in India and the Nile in Egypt). Not so with Israel. To the Israelites, the Jordan River was a barrier — an obstacle to be crossed in order to reach the land God had promised to give them. In fact, this perspective is the source of our expression "to cross the Jordan," which means to pass through something that stands in the way.

How did the Jordan River get this reputation? It started before God's people entered the Promised Land.

From all the earth's inhabitants, God chose the descendants of Abraham to be his people, his witnesses to the world. God would give them a land to live in, and they in turn were to live according to his ways so that the whole world could see what happens when a group of people live for God with all their hearts. After leaving Egypt and establishing their covenant with God at Mount Sinai, the Israelites reached the land east of the Jordan. They were poised to enter the Promised Land, but they were afraid to venture in and possess it. As punishment for their unbelief, God sent them back into the wilderness to wander for forty years.

When their time of wandering was over, they once again camped on the east side of the Jordan River, near Jericho, ready to possess the land. But the river was at flood stage! Imagine how the people must have felt.

No doubt this timing pleased the Canaanites. They worshiped fertility gods, particularly Baal, whom they believed to be the god of water, rain, storm, wind, thunder, and lightning. In their minds, the flooded river demonstrated Baal's protection. God, however, was about to show that he alone is God and that he alone commands the forces of nature.

When the Israelites broke camp, the priests walked ahead of them carrying the ark of the covenant, in which God's presence resided. The moment the priests stepped into the river, God stopped the water from flowing. The priests stood on dry ground in the middle of the riverbed while all the Israelites passed by. In this session, we'll explore the significance of this miraculous river crossing — for the Israelites and for Christians today.

Opening Thoughts (4 minutes)

The Very Words of God

"For the LORD your God dried up the Jordan before you until you had crossed over. The LORD your God did to the Jordan just what he had done to the Red Sea ... so that all the peoples of the earth might know that the hand of the LORD is powerful and so that you might always fear the LORD your God."

Joshua 4:23 – 24

Think About It

When we make a commitment to live for God, it doesn't mean we won't encounter obstacles between us and the work God has called us to accomplish. The key to living by faith, however, lies in how we respond to those barriers.

What barriers do you think stand between Christians today and the work God wants us to accomplish? To what extent do we commit ourselves to God and step out in faith to do what he has called us to do? What keeps us from completely trusting him?

DVD Teaching Notes (17 minutes)

Discovering the Jordan River

Understanding what the Jordan meant to the Israelites

Exploring the meaning of Jesus' baptism in the Jordan

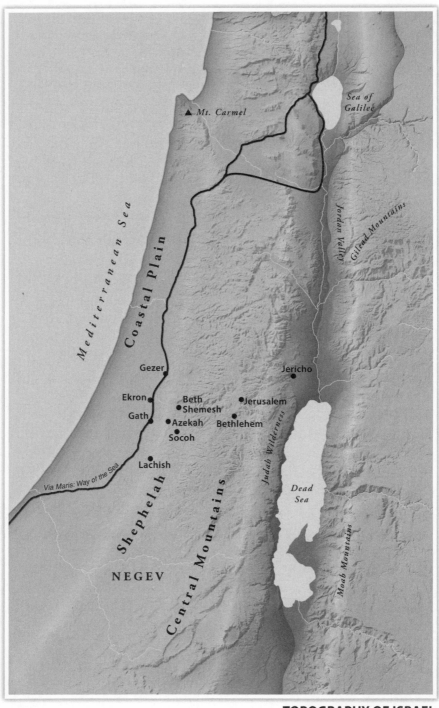

TOPOGRAPHY OF ISRAEL

DVD Discussion (7 minutes)

1. When we read or hear about events in the Bible that occurred near the Jordan River, most of us have our own image of what the river looks like. What surprised you when you actually saw the river in the video?

   In what ways does knowing the truth about the river change your understanding of events recorded in the Bible?

2. What did God demonstrate and to whom when he miraculously stopped the flowing waters of the Jordan River so that the Israelites could cross it?

3. What similar meanings do you see in the Israelites' crossing of the Jordan River in order to possess the Promised Land and Jesus' baptism in the Jordan?

DATA FILE
The Jordan River

- Received its name from a Hebrew word that means "to descend, to go down."
- Starts more than 1,500 feet above sea level at the foot of Mount Hermon (elevation 9,000 feet) in northern Israel and ends almost 1,400 feet below sea level at the Dead Sea.
- Meanders for 200 miles from Mount Hermon to the Dead Sea—about 90 miles as the crow flies.
- Flows through the Great Rift Valley, a cut in the earth's crust extending all the way to Lake Victoria in southern Africa.
- Is one of the fastest-flowing rivers in the world for its size.
- Is dammed up where it runs out of the Sea of Galilee to help meet the water needs of present-day Israel.

JORDAN RIVER

Small Group Bible Discovery and Discussion (21 minutes)

Learning to Cross the Jordan

The first time the Israelites were poised to cross the Jordan, they refused (Numbers 14:1 – 4). They considered the obstacles they saw before them to be too great. They feared the challenges ahead more than they feared the Lord their God, so they wavered when he called them to step out in faith and possess the land. After forty years of wandering in the desert and learning to depend on God, the Israelites once again camped on the east side of the Jordan, prepared to cross into the Promised Land.

1. What kind of report did the spies (other than Joshua and Caleb) bring back from their exploration of the land of Canaan? (See Numbers 13:27 – 32.)

    What impact did their testimony have on the people? (See Numbers 14:1 – 4.)

    Who was ready to get their feet wet, and why? (See Numbers 14:6 – 9.)

2. The second time Israel was poised to enter the Promised Land, Joshua sent out two spies. Notice how their report (Joshua 2:23 – 24) differed from the first report. Who was ready to get their feet wet?

3. Read the instructions given to the people when it was time to cross the Jordan. (See Joshua 3:1 - 5.)

   a. Why was the ark to go ahead of them?

   b. What did Joshua tell the people God would do for them?

   c. Why would these instructions have been important to people who were about to step out in faith and cross the Jordan?

4. What was God saying to the Israelites when he miraculously enabled them to cross the Jordan River? (See Joshua 3:9 - 11.)

   What impact do you think this had on them when they faced barriers on the other side of the Jordan River?

5. What special message did God reveal to Joshua, and why would it have been important to Joshua and to the people? (See Joshua 3:7 - 8.)

6. Why do you think God explained in such detail what he was going to do and why he would do it?

What do you think the Israelites needed to remember or discover about God? About themselves?

Faith Lesson (5 minutes)

The Israelites viewed the Jordan River as a barrier between them and the Promised Land where God had called them to live. As Christians, we also face obstacles that stand between us and the work to which God has called us. Like the ancient Israelites, we also are often reluctant to step out in faith and follow God.

1. Imagine yourself standing on the bank of the Jordan River, looking toward the land on the far side that represents your life's mission or a specific task God has given to you. What in this picture is your "Jordan River," the frightening barrier that keeps you from fully plunging ahead into the life God intends for you?

2. Why is this barrier stopping you from taking possession of the "land" God has given to you?

3. What if you were to step out in faith believing that God will
    be faithful to lead and protect you through whatever lies
    ahead?

    How might this affect your belief in God?

    Your witness to other people?

    Your willingness to keep "getting your feet wet"?

Closing (1 minute)

Obstacles always have the potential to strike fear into the hearts of
God's people. But over and over again God has promised to be with
those who are totally committed to him. Read 2 Chronicles 20:17
aloud: "You will not have to fight this battle. Take up your positions;
stand firm and see the deliverance the LORD will give you, O Judah
and Jerusalem. Do not be afraid; do not be discouraged. Go out to
face them tomorrow, and the LORD will be with you."

Then pray, asking God to help you "cross the Jordan" and be the influence in your culture that he wants you to be. Thank him for his love
and faithfulness. Seek his help in facing the obstacles that lie ahead of
you so that others will see your life and know that he is God.

Memorize

*You will not have to fight this battle. Take up your positions; stand firm and
see the deliverance the LORD will give you, O Judah and Jerusalem. Do not be
afraid; do not be discouraged. Go out to face them tomorrow, and the LORD
will be with you.*

2 Chronicles 20:17

Making God Known to the World

In-Depth Personal Bible Study Sessions

Day One | Following the God of All

The Very Words of God

> *The* LORD *himself goes before you and will be with you; he will never leave you nor forsake you. Do not be afraid; do not be discouraged.*
>
> **Deuteronomy 31:8**

Bible Discovery

The Ark of God

The ark of the covenant was the focal point of God's presence among his people. The cloud of God's glory would regularly appear above the mercy seat of the ark, so to come before the ark was to enter into the very presence of God. To the people of Israel, the ark was the physical evidence that the holy, sovereign, mighty God of Abraham was with them.

DATA FILE
The Ark of the Covenant

The ark of the covenant was so important that before God described any other sacred object—including the tabernacle—he described in detail how the ark was to be constructed. The ark:

- Was made of extremely hard acacia wood common to the Sinai Peninsula.
- Was three feet nine inches long, two feet three inches wide, and two feet three inches tall.
- Was gold plated and had a gold rim around the top.

continued on next page . . .

- Stood on four legs, and on each side were two gold rings in which poles were inserted so the Levites (the priestly tribe) could carry it.
- Had a cover—called the mercy or atonement seat—made of pure gold. On top of the cover were two cherubim—probably sphinxes—whose wings stretched over the cover.
- Was viewed by the Israelites as God's footstool (1 Chronicles 28:2) and focal point of God's presence and glory among his people (Numbers 14:43–44; Psalm 132:7–8).

1. Read Exodus 25:10–22, which describes the construction of the ark of the covenant, and note the two purposes God intended it to serve (vv. 16, 22).

2. Why was it dangerous to approach the ark of the covenant? (See Leviticus 16:1–2.)

   Who was permitted to approach the ark of the covenant, when, and for what purpose? (See Leviticus 16:3, 17.)

3. What evidence do we see that in the eyes of Israel the ark of the covenant truly represented God's presence on earth? (See Joshua 7:6–9; Judges 20:26–28; Psalm 99:1–3.)

4. Notice where the ark was carried when the Israelites began
   to cross the Jordan River (Joshua 3:1 – 6, 14 – 17) and during
   the siege of Jericho (Joshua 6:1 – 14). What did this place-
   ment of the ark symbolize?

   God could have divided the Jordan River or destroyed the
   city of Jericho at any time. Why do you think he waited to
   act until the priests carrying the ark of the covenant entered
   the swift-flowing water and until the ark had been carried
   around Jericho for seven days?

5. Long after Israel crossed the Jordan River, the people and
   even the priests of God became unfaithful and dishonored
   God. First Samuel 4 records a dark chapter in the history of
   Israel when God removed his presence from Israel because
   of their disobedience.

   a. What did the ark mean to Israel, and what was its reputa-
      tion among the Philistines?

   b. What did the Israelites depend on to save them? Why do
      you think their efforts failed?

   c. Why do you think God allowed the ark of the covenant
      to be captured, and what message do you think this sent
      to Israel?

DID YOU KNOW?

Following ancient Near Eastern custom, God instructed Moses to make two summary documents of the covenant God had made with his people. These documents (each of which contained all Ten Commandments) were his guarantee that his Word would never fail. Normally, each party took a summary copy of the covenant and placed it in their most sacred place, where it would be read regularly as a reminder of the covenant. God, however, gave both copies to Moses and ordered him to place them into the ark. Imagine how Moses reacted when he realized that the most sacred place for God and for Israel was the same — the ark of the covenant! That is why the ark represented to Israel the very presence of God.

Reflection

It was no coincidence that the ark, which represented the presence of God on earth, went before the Israelites into Canaan. To Israel, it meant that God was going before them into the land. It meant something to the Canaanites as well. As explained in the video: "The flood waters of the Jordan River represented their god Baal's protection. By dividing the Jordan River so that the Israelites could pass through, God was making a powerful declaration that he not only was stronger than the forces of nature, but that he was more powerful than the gods of the culture."

In what ways does the image of the ark going before the Israelites encourage your actions of faith and trust in God, particularly when the barriers before you seem impossible to overcome?

How might what happened to Israel after their unfaithfulness (1 Samuel 2:27 – 36; 4:1 – 22) apply to Christians today if we indulge in the sins of the same culture we are to influence for God?

For the Israelites, the ark represented God's presence among them. According to 1 Corinthians 3:16 – 17, where does God reveal his presence today? How should this affect your attitudes and actions? Your relationships with unbelievers?

THINK ABOUT IT

During Israel's wilderness wanderings, God performed many miracles in relationship to water. When the Israelites crossed the Jordan River, they entered a land where the people worshiped Baal as the god of water, rain, storm, wind, thunder, and lightning. Surely the miraculous crossing of the Jordan must have impressed on them that their God was not just the God of the desert, but that he was God of everything.

If you had been an Israelite on the day God stopped the waters of the Jordan River, what might you have thought about the God you served? If you had been a Canaanite on that day, what might you have thought about your future and the people entering your land?

Day Two | Go Where God Wants You to Go

The Very Words of God

> *I have set the LORD always before me. Because he is at my right hand, I will not be shaken.*
>
> *Psalm 16:8*

Bible Discovery

Choose Wisely When You Face the Jordan

Every day we choose how we will respond to the obstacles before us. Often God calls his people to step out in faith and face the obstacles head-on, not knowing exactly what the result will be. When the priests stepped boldly into the rushing waters of the Jordan River, for example, they didn't know what God would do, but they chose to be totally dependent on his promise. In response, God demonstrated his power and faithfulness to a watching world.

The choices we make when we "face the Jordan" make a difference. Each of the following Bible passages tells a story involving choices God's people made in relationship to (or in close proximity to) the Jordan River. Read each story and note the following:

- • Why people made the choices they did
- • What their choices reveal about themselves and their commitment to God
- • What kind of impact their choices had (on themselves, on future generations, on the watching world)

Genesis 13:5 – 18

Deuteronomy 1:20 – 37; 34:1 – 4

2 Samuel 17:16 – 22

1 Kings 16:29 – 33; 17:1 – 6

2 Kings 2:1 – 15

DID YOU KNOW?

The Jordan River does not flow through a valley carved by water. Rather, it flows through a rift, or cut, in the earth's crust. So the soil of the Jordan valley is not the rich soil that results from repeated flooding; it is sediment that settled from an ancient sea. It absorbs little water and doesn't sustain vegetation.

Along the river's edge, however, the soil does support vegetation and a dense tangle of lush growth thrives there. For this reason, an area that appears from a distance to be fertile is actually barren. So when "Lot looked up and saw that the whole plain of the Jordan was well watered, like the garden of the Lord" (Genesis 13:10), it is likely that the thickets of the Jordan attracted his attention. But "well watered" does not mean the soil can support flocks or agriculture. In fact, with the exception of a few oases like Jericho, where springs have washed the salt out of the soil, the plain of the Jordan supports little life.

THICKETS OF THE JORDAN

Reflection

When the Israelites reached the Jordan River, they had to choose whether or not they would be totally committed to God. They had to choose whether anything — including fast-flowing water — was outside of God's control and influence. They had to decide whether they would put their faith in God and trust him to lead them through the unknown or put their trust in what they could see.

Faith is not a "half-Baal and a half-God relationship." Consider the obstacles you face to be like the Jordan River — the place where God demonstrates his power, presence, and protection. Have you, in faith, crossed the "Jordan"? Are you on the side of the "Jordan" where God wants you to be? What dangers do you face if you "stay on the bank" when God has called you to cross the Jordan?

Have you made a total commitment to God and in faith given your life to Jesus Christ? If not, what's holding you back? Which barrier is keeping you from making a total commitment to God?

If we are totally committed to God, we cannot allow anything to stand between us and God's calling. How willing are you to take whatever steps God calls you to take, even if it means crossing (and perhaps recrossing) the "Jordan"?

Memorize

Turn my heart toward your statutes and not toward selfish gain. Turn my eyes away from worthless things; preserve my life according to your word.

Psalm 119:36 – 37

THINK ABOUT IT
Deceived by Appearances

As Lot surveyed the Great Rift Valley from the edge of the Judah Wilderness near Bethel, the green thickets of the Jordan (Jeremiah 49:19; Zechariah 11:3) looked promising. In an arid land, who wouldn't want to live near a flowing river? So he shrewdly chose for himself what appeared to be the best land. As we know from Scripture, however, the obvious choice isn't always the best one—nor is it the one that pleases God.

When Lot left Abraham, he not only left the wilderness, where a person had to depend on God for survival, but he also left Abraham's God. That, in turn, spelled disaster for Lot and his family. Because the watered portion of the riverbed was too small and dense for his flocks and the adjacent plains were unable to sustain life, Lot had to move. His solution was to settle in the well-watered, pagan city of Sodom among a people who worshiped Canaanite fertility gods and practiced all forms of sexual perversion.

Eventually Lot "sat in the gate" as a leader among the people of Sodom. Only God's mercy and the loyalty of his uncle Abraham allowed him and his daughters to escape God's judgment on the evil city. After losing everything else dear to him, including his wife, Lot discovered that even his daughters had become like the people of Sodom (Genesis 19:30–38). His grandchildren became the people of Moab and Ammon, infamous in the Bible for their idolatry and evil ways.

Perhaps we ought to consider if Lot's story is as far removed from our lives as we might think. Just as the poor soil of the Great Rift Valley, through which the Jordan River flows, seemed suitable for grazing when Lot first looked at it, our culture's values and practices can appear desirable and healthful. It can be very easy for us to be caught up in them. After all, most of us choose our entertainment, music, jobs, food, and even our wardrobes according to what the world deems attractive.

So how is it possible for us to participate actively in our culture, yet make choices according to God's standards—choices that please him? How do we avoid being deceived into choosing what appears to be attractive and harmless but is actually harmful?

Day Three | "Wet Feet": Sign of Total Commitment

The Very Words of God

This is what the LORD says — he who created you, O Jacob, he who formed you, O Israel:"Fear not, for I have redeemed you; I have summoned you by name; you are mine. When you pass through the waters, I will be with you; and when you pass through the rivers, they will not sweep over you."

Isaiah 43:1 – 2

Bible Discovery

Taking the Step of Total Commitment

When the priests of Israel stepped into the flooded Jordan River, they were making a total commitment to trust God. God responded to their step of faith in a powerful, miraculous way. But we need to remember that the Jordan River parted for God's people only after they made the first move, after they took that challenging step of faith.

To better understand what it means to get "wet feet" and make a total commitment to God, consider the example of the following people in the Bible who also took challenging steps of faith:

Gideon (Judges 6:11 – 24, 36 – 40; 7:1 – 22)
When challenged to get his feet wet, how did Gideon respond? What did he learn as God continued to place challenges before him?

Rahab (Joshua 2:1 – 21; 6:22 – 25; Hebrews 11:31)
In what way(s) did she get "wet feet," and what impact did her actions have?

Jonathan and his armor-bearer (1 Samuel 14:4–15, 20–23)

How did God use their courageous act of faith?

Widow at Zarephath (1 Kings 17:7–16)

What was at stake for her?

Elijah (1 Kings 18:15–34)

As a result of his faith, how did God's people respond?

Shadrach, Meshach, and Abednego (Daniel 3:1–29)

How was God glorified as a result of their faith? What impact did their step of faith have on a watching world?

Reflection

If we take seriously our responsibility to be a positive influence in our culture, we must be totally committed to God. In order for God's power to be released in our lives, we must step out in faith and be willing to get our feet wet.

What "test of faith" has challenged you in the past, and how did you respond? Did you learn anything that would lead you to respond differently today?

What impact has getting "wet feet" and seeing God work as a result had on your spiritual growth? Why?

What step of faith might God want you, your family, and/or your church to take so that he can be more visible in your community? How much would you have to depend on God if you were to take that step?

Memorize

Faith is being sure of what we hope for and certain of what we do not see. This is what the ancients were commended for.

Hebrews 11:1 – 2

Day Four | Up, Out of the Jordan

The Very Words of God

Here is my servant, whom I uphold, my chosen one in whom I delight; I will put my Spirit on him and he will bring justice to the nations.

Isaiah 42:1

Bible Discovery

The Baptism of Jesus: Ushering in a New Order

The greatest New Testament event to take place in relationship to the Jordan River was the baptism of Jesus. The gospel accounts tell us that the Holy Spirit, in bodily form like a dove, descended from heaven and hovered over Jesus as he was baptized. The image of the dove hovering above Jesus is also similar to the hovering of God's Spirit over the watery chaos before the creation of the world.

Read the following Scripture texts and consider the parallels between the symbolism of Jesus' baptism and the creation story:

	The Text	The Parallels
The Water	Gen. 1:2	Before creation, the watery deep was formless and represented chaos.
	Matt. 3:16	Jesus descended into the water, which represented chaos and death.
The Spirit	Gen. 1:2	At creation, the Spirit hovered and moved over the water.
	Matt. 3:16	The Spirit of God, represented by the dove, descended on Jesus and moved with him.
God's Approval	Gen. 1:31	After creating the world, God was pleased with his creation.
	Matt. 3:17	After Jesus' baptism, God was pleased with his Son, Jesus.
A New Creation	Gen. 1:3–30	Out of the formless void, God made a new world that had never existed before.
	Matt. 11:2–5	As Jesus came up out of the Jordan, he ushered in a new creation, a new world order in which love and healing would prevail over evil.
Temptation	Gen. 3:1–7	Soon after creation, Satan tempted Adam and Eve.
	Matt. 4:1–11	Immediately after his baptism, Jesus was led into the wilderness to face Satan's temptations.

DID YOU KNOW?

Although many Christians today recognize the dove as a symbol of God's presence and approval during the baptism of Jesus, the people of Jesus' day seem to have made a different connection. They seem to have recognized similarities between Jesus' baptism and the creation of the world. Just as the Spirit hovered over the watery chaos that preceded the creation of the world, the Spirit hovering above Jesus symbolized the new creation that he was ushering in. By mirroring the creation account during Jesus' baptism, God revealed Jesus' calling: he was God's Son, the Messiah, sent to usher in a new order.

Reflection

When John the Baptist wanted to know if Jesus really was the one God had sent, Jesus simply replied, "The blind receive sight, the lame walk, those who have leprosy are cured, the deaf hear, the dead are raised, and the good news is preached to the poor" (Matthew 11:5).

In what ways were the actions of Jesus as he went about his ministry evidence of a new creation, a new order, a new way of doing things?

Why do you think Jesus responded to John in this way? And what do you think his response meant to John?

Think back to when the Israelites came up out of the Jordan and went into the Promised Land. In what ways were they also ushering in a new order? What did God intend the evidence of that new order to be?

Memorize

Now if you obey me fully and keep my covenant, then out of all nations you will be my treasured possession. Although the whole earth is mine, you will be for me a kingdom of priests and a holy nation.

Exodus 19:5–6a

Day Five | Ambassadors of a New Order

The Very Words of God

We are therefore Christ's ambassadors, as though God were making his appeal through us.

2 Corinthians 5:20

Bible Discovery

Followers of Jesus Are Called to Be God's Ambassadors

Jesus' baptism in the Jordan River symbolized God's creation of a new order — a new, loving, caring way of doing things that the Spirit of God was bringing to the world. As followers of Jesus, we are God's ambassadors. In a world that does not understand or practice the values that Jesus taught and lived, we have been given the job of demonstrating those values. We are called to bring his healing, love, and comfort into the lives of broken people.

1. What surprising thing did Jesus say about his followers in Luke 7:28?

   What does this say to you about your job as an ambassador of God?

Think of a specific time when, because of God's Spirit living within you, you demonstrated who God is to someone
else. Why would it be correct to say that you did something
greater than John, who preceded the coming of the new creation Jesus instituted?

2. In John 14:5 – 13, Jesus speaks about his calling and explains
    what his disciples also are called to do.

    a. What did Jesus say he was here to do?

    b. What did he say those who have faith in him are to do?

    c. How do both of these callings compare to what God
        called the Israelites to do in the Promised Land?

    d. What surprising thing did Jesus say about what his fol-
        lowers would do and why? (See verse 12.)

3. How important is it to Jesus for his followers to obey God's calling and be ambassadors of his new order? (See Matthew 25:31 – 46.)

Reflection

The new order, which Jesus ushered in after his baptism, brings hope, healing, and love to our broken world. The degree to which we actually bring about this new order is the degree to which we successfully impact our culture for God's glory.

What are the implications of being an ambassador of Jesus' new creation? As a parent? A spouse? A neighbor? A church member? An employee or employer? A community leader?

How consistently are you — an ambassador of Christ — bringing healing, love, integrity, sympathy, and truth to your community? How consistently are you shedding materialism and exhibiting the peace and joy that come from storing up heavenly treasure?

As Matthew 25:34 – 40 indicates, the new creation is marked by ministering to those in need, standing for justice for the innocent, and bringing Jesus' healing and restoring love to these people. In which specific issues, concerns, problems, or for which individuals in your community would God have you serve as his ambassador? What steps of faith must you take to obey God and bring him honor in these specific areas?

Pray that Jesus, who is at the right hand of the Father, will help you be his ambassador in your world. Ask him to help you reach out to the poor, the hurting, the sick, and the spiritually blind. Ask him for the courage to step out in faith, to confront any obstacle that would hinder you, and to live in such a way that others will see the Father.

FIRST FRUITS

In this video, you'll discover some of the fascinating history of Jericho — the lowest (located more than a thousand feet below sea level) and oldest (dating back to more than 8000 BC) city in the world. The tel of Jericho stands at the opening of a mountain pass near the northern end of the Dead Sea. Elisha's Spring still flows as it has for thousands of years, making Jericho a beautiful, lush oasis in the Jordan Valley.

During Bible times, the fortified city of Jericho was on the strategic road linking the Via Maris and the King's Highway — the major trade routes of the ancient world. So it should not surprise us to learn that Jericho played a prominent role in various Bible stories and events.

After forty years of wilderness wandering, the Israelites were ready to possess Canaan, the land God promised them. They traveled up from the Negev Desert, then continued north, east of the Dead Sea. Because Jericho was their first obstacle in possessing the Promised Land, Israel sent spies into the city where Rahab, a prostitute, protected them from capture by the king of Jericho. After telling the spies how afraid her people became when they heard the Israelites were approaching, Rahab confessed that "the LORD your God is God in heaven above and on earth below." Clearly the Israelites were demonstrating by their conduct that God is God. Because of her faith, Rahab and her family were saved from the destruction of Jericho, and she became one of four women God mentions in the ancestral lineage of Jesus the Messiah!

The battle for Jericho clearly was God's battle. God orchestrated his will, using the obedient Israelites as his instruments. He brought about a miraculous victory that caused the pagan

Canaanites to fear Israel's God even more. He also wanted the Israelites to remember that everything they had — including the victory over Jericho — came from him, and to trust him to continue to provide for them. So after Jericho fell, God required Israel to leave Jericho's ruins as their "first fruits" offering to him. The ruins were to be left as a testimony that the land belonged to God and that those who lived in it sought to serve him.

The story of Jericho is a reminder that God has called us — his people — to be holy people. He has not provided for us purely for our benefit. He has given us what we have for his service and glory. May we never forget that what has been set apart for God belongs to him — and him alone.

Opening Thoughts (4 minutes)

The Very Words of God

> O LORD, you are my God; I will exalt you and praise your name, for in perfect faithfulness you have done marvelous things, things planned long ago. You have made the city a heap of rubble, the fortified town a ruin, the foreigners' stronghold a city no more; it will never be rebuilt.
>
> Isaiah 25:1 – 2

Think About It

As Christians today, we readily give assent to God's supremacy and sovereignty. We are quick to agree that the whole earth and everything in it is his. But to what extent do we really live that way as we go about daily life?

How much of who we are do we realize comes from the hand of God?

How much of what we accomplish do we realize is enabled by the hand of God?

How much of what we possess do we recognize as a gift from the hand of God?

DVD Teaching Notes (16 minutes)

Jericho: city with an important past

Rahab's unusual faith

God reveals his battle strategy

First fruits: set apart for God's purpose

DVD Discussion (8 minutes)

1. For what reasons was Jericho a strategic city during ancient times?

2. What message(s) about himself do you think God was conveying through events related to the ancient city of Jericho — from before the spies went into the city, through its destruction, and even in the fact that ancient Jericho remains in ruins today?

3. What is the principle of "first fruits," and in what ways has your understanding of this important biblical principle been influenced by the material presented in the video?

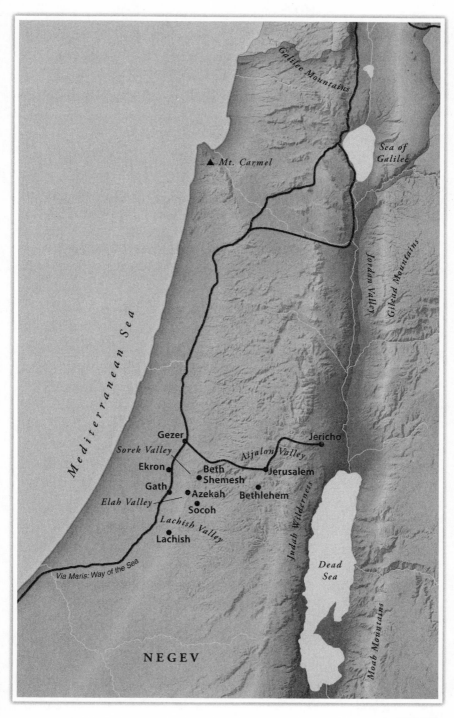

ISRAEL

THINK ABOUT IT

It's amazing to realize that the traffic going through the modern city of Jericho exists for many of the same reasons that ancient Jericho was built. The land of Israel is mountainous, as is the land east of the Jordan River. There are very few routes for crossing these mountains from the west or the east, but one such crossroad is near the northern end of the Dead Sea just west of Jericho. So in ancient times, the road through Jericho connected the main trade routes between Egypt and Mesopotamia: the Via Maris on the coastal plain on the far side of the mountains west of Jericho and the King's Highway east of the mountains of Moab and Gilead.

Its strategic location obviously has made Jericho an important city for a long time. But there are other reasons people settled there. Jericho has a warm, sunny climate all year long. Elisha's Spring keeps the city green and inviting compared to the rest of the Jordan River Valley. For thousands of years these characteristics have made it a desirable place to live. Evidence shows that it existed in 8300 BC and may be even older. Consider that when Abraham settled in the land, Jericho had already been in existence for seven thousand years!

JERICHO

Small Group Bible Discovery and Discussion (21 minutes)

The Battle Belongs to the Lord

After crossing the Jordan River, the Israelites needed to conquer Jericho, the gateway to the Promised Land. During that first encounter, they learned crucial lessons about fighting God's battles and what it meant to acknowledge that God had given them all they had and to trust that he would continue to meet their needs.

1. All of Israel camped on the plains of Jericho and prepared to possess the land God had promised them. While they were waiting for God's direction, who appeared to Joshua, and how did Joshua respond to him? (See Joshua 5:13 – 14.)

   If you had been in Joshua's shoes, preparing Israel to fight against the fortified city of Jericho, what would you have thought when you realized that the commander of the army of the Lord had actually come to be with you?

2. In Joshua 6:1 – 6, God gives Joshua his marching orders. What was unusual about the battle strategy God laid out?

   From a human perspective, would this strategy work? Would you have been able to convince your army to approach a crucial battle in this way? Why or why not?

3. In what ways did God clearly communicate that victory in this battle belonged to him? (See Joshua 5:14; 6:2.)

4. What did Joshua and Israel do that showed they understood that the battle for Jericho belonged to the Lord? (See Joshua 6:6 – 21, 24.)

Faith Lesson (5 minutes)

Although Christians today usually don't face battles involving armed conflict as the Israelites did at Jericho, it certainly is intimidating to stand against the powerful, well-established strongholds of evil in our culture. Like the children of Israel, we must choose whether or not we will follow God's calling and participate in the battle for his kingdom — at work, at school, at home, and in the larger community.

If we truly believe the battle we are called to fight belongs to God, how does that affect:

Our desire to know him, to listen to him, and to learn his strategy?

Our commitment to obey him completely (even if we think there must be a better way)?

Our recognition of his provision for us and our trust that he will continue to provide for our needs in the future?

DID YOU NOTICE?

In Hebrew, "Joshua" and "Jesus" are the same name — *Yeshua*, which means "the Lord [Yahweh] saves." It is interesting to consider how each of them demonstrated God's saving power in the vicinity of Jericho. Notice the similarities between what Joshua did to open up Jericho, the gateway to the Promised Land, and what Jesus did as he made his journey toward death to open the gateway to heaven, the new "Promised Land."

What Happened	Joshua	Jesus
Came in God's name	Josh. 6:1–7, 15–17	Luke 19:9–10
Displayed obedience	Josh. 6:15–21, 24	Luke 18:31–33
Saved an outcast	Josh. 6:22–25	Luke 19:5–10
Led others to recognize that the Lord is God	Josh. 3:9–11	Luke 18:35–43

Closing (1 minute)

On Mount Sinai, before the people of Israel reached the Promised Land, God said, "I am making a covenant with you. Before all your people I will do wonders never before done in any nation in all the world. The people you live among will see how awesome is the work that I, the LORD, will do for you. Obey what I command you today" (Exodus 34:10–11).

God's desire to show himself to the world through people who will obey him has not changed. If you are willing to follow God's battle plan, to impact your culture as powerfully as the ancient Israelites who faithfully walked around Jericho thirteen times, then invite him to help you live for him in whatever situation you face. Thank him for his faithfulness, his indwelling presence within you as a Christian, and his Word — the Bible. Ask him to help you know him and live for him every day.

Memorize

Then the LORD said, "I am making a covenant with you. Before all your people I will do wonders never before done in any nation in all the world. The people you live among will see how awesome is the work that I, the LORD, will do for you. Obey what I command you today."

Exodus 34:10 – 11

Making God Known to the World

In-Depth Personal Study Sessions

Day One | Called to Be Holy

The Very Words of God

> *You are a people holy to the Lord your God. Out of all the peoples on the face of the earth, the Lord has chosen you to be his treasured possession.*
>
> **Deuteronomy 14:2**

Bible Discovery

God's Love of Holiness

The conquest of Canaan and the destruction of cities such as Jericho pose an ethical dilemma for many Bible readers. How could the God of love and mercy demand such merciless destruction of the inhabitants of the Promised Land? Although none of us can completely understand the sovereign God of the universe, the Bible reveals much about how seriously God views sin.

1. What kind of a world did God create from the chaos of water? (See Genesis 1 - 2, especially 1:2, 31.)

2. How did Adam and Eve — the crown of God's creation — respond to God in the garden of Eden? (See Genesis 3:1 - 12.)

3. What has God always wanted his people to be? (See Exodus
    19:5 - 6; Joshua 24:19 - 23; Leviticus 11:44; 1 Peter 1:15 - 16;
    2:9 - 10.)

4. In contrast to the Israelites, who were called to be holy
    before God, what were the pagan inhabitants of Canaan like?
    (See Leviticus 18:1 - 5, 24 - 30; Deuteronomy 18:9 - 13.)

THE TRUTH OF THE MATTER

Throughout the Old Testament, God addressed the topic of holiness. Because
the Israelites were his chosen people, he challenged them to obey him, to
hate sin, and to avoid becoming like the sinful people around them. Today,
God still calls his people to be holy. That is why Christians are to obey his
commands and resist the Evil One. If you haven't already done so, take time
to study the Bible's emphasis on holiness. The following passages will help
you discover God's perspective.

Scripture Text	How God Views Sin
Ex. 32:1, 7 – 14, 31 – 35	
Lev. 26:14 – 1	
Num. 15:32 – 40	

Deut. 7:25–26	
Ps. 11:4–7	
Prov. 15:8–9, 26, 29	
Jer. 44:2–6	

Reflection

God is a holy God. The prophet Isaiah described him as being "exalted by his justice" and shown "holy by his righteousness" (Isaiah 5:16). And David honored God as "the Holy One ... the praise of Israel" (Psalm 22:3). So it is no wonder that God hates all sin and honors those who are blameless in his sight.

> What part does holiness play in loving "the LORD your God with all your heart and with all your soul and with all your strength" (Deuteronomy 6:5)?

> Although God calls every Christian to be holy, we still live in a sinful world with sinful people. How do you balance being involved enough to influence your culture for God without allowing yourself to be drawn into the sinfulness around you?

What is your personal commitment to being holy before God, and what lifestyle changes do you need to make in order to live out this commitment?

What is the difference between trying to be "holy" in your own sight and strength and asking God to fill you with his Spirit and empower you to love him and hate sin?

Memorize

> *Praise be to the God and Father of our Lord Jesus Christ, who ... chose us in him before the creation of the world to be holy and blameless in his sight.*
>
> *Ephesians 1:3–4*

Day Two | When God's Judgment Falls

The Very Words of God

> *You are not a God who takes pleasure in evil; with you the wicked cannot dwell.*
>
> *Psalm 5:4*

Bible Discovery

The Price of Sin

As much as we may like to think otherwise, sin comes at a price that cannot be ignored. As great as God's love is, he will not tolerate evil. To do so would be a denial of his very character.

1. Look up the following Bible passages and describe what you discover about God's response to and judgment of sin.

Scripture Text	God's Response and Judgment
Gen. 6:5–9, 13–14, 17–18; 7:23	
Gen. 18:20–33; 19:1, 12–13, 24–25	
Num. 16:1–11, 20–35	
Num. 25:1–9	
Rev. 20:7–10	

2. As the Israelites prepared to battle pagan nations in the Promised Land, what instructions did God give his people concerning their attacks on cities such as Jericho? (See Deuteronomy 7:16; 20:16 - 18; Joshua 6:16 - 18, 21 - 24.)

    Why did he give these instructions?

Do you think God's commands were easy for the Israelites to follow? Why or why not?

Would they have been easy for you to follow?

DATA FILE
The Judgment of God

The judgment of God (called *cherem* in Hebrew) is translated "totally devoted to God" or "utterly destroyed." In modern English, we might say "damned." Only such total judgment could remove the pollution of sin so that God's creation would once again honor him.

The Bible provides several examples of God's *cherem* falling on sinful people:

- Genesis 6–8 — God flooded the entire earth to wash away a perverse human race.
- Genesis 19 — God poured fire and brimstone on the evil cities of Sodom and Gomorrah.
- Numbers 16 — Because they defied him, God destroyed Korah, Dathan, Abiram, and their followers, as well as all of their family members and belongings.

The conquest of Canaan was a step in God's plan to reclaim his world. Only the total destruction of the sinful Canaanites would make the land fit for his people to serve him and enable them to be a blessing to all nations so that the world would know that Yahweh is God. To bring about his judgment and restoration, God chose as his instruments the same creatures who had sinned against him.

3. What did the Israelites carry as they marched around Jericho, and what were they acknowledging by doing this? (See
   Joshua 6:6 – 9.)

4. What similarities do you notice between Joshua 6:15 – 16, 20
   and 1 Thessalonians 4:16?

Reflection

Although God abhors sin more than we can possibly imagine, he
also has provided a way of forgiveness, redemption, and purification
from all unrighteousness (John 3:16; 1 John 1:9).

Based on what you are learning in these studies, how would you
respond to someone who claims that a loving God could not
have killed so many people in Canaan — both pagans and Israelites who persisted in sin?

In light of what you are learning about how seriously God views
sin, how important is it for you to deal with even the "small" sins
in your life? What are those sins, and are you willing to turn away
from them?

In what way(s) is sin influencing your relationship with
God? Your relationships with other people? Your witness of
who God is to the world?

DATA FILE
The Holy, the Common, and the Abominable

The Old Testament's view of sin and judgment produced a concept of
reality divided into three parts: the holy, the common, and the abominable
(unclean).

The Holy

Anything devoted to Yahweh or used in his service was considered holy.
God made some things, such as the Sabbath, holy. Some things became
holy (such as first fruits) because they were offered to God in service. Once
something had been given to God, it was his alone.

The worst kind of sin was to use something holy for one's personal benefit.
Jericho had been given to God, so it was not to be inhabited again. Israel, as
a nation, had been set apart to serve God, so the people were not to worship anyone or anything else. And according to the New Testament, every
Christian is holy, set apart to serve God. So we must not serve any other
person, idea, or thing. Every part of our lives should be dedicated to serving
the Lord—including our occupations, families, and recreation. We are to
do nothing for our benefit alone. To do so is to place ourselves under God's
judgment.

The Common

In the Old Testament, things belonging to people were considered common:
household possessions, animals, land, and so on. These were to be used in
godly ways, but they were under the stewardship of those who had them. In
the New Testament, however, the holy and common were joined. Everything,
even the mundane, is now to be used in God's service.

The prophet Zechariah said that when the Messiah returns, even the bowls used in family cooking will be as sacred as those used in temple worship. "And on that day there will no longer be a Canaanite in the house of the LORD Almighty" (Zechariah 14:20–21). That is the story of Jericho. The Canaanites living there had so polluted God's land that they had to be removed by his judgment. Then the holy people of God could begin to find ways to serve him in every part of their lives.

The Abominable

God detests abominations—anything associated with the worship of other gods and any behavior that perverts the lifestyle God intends human beings to live. Leviticus 18 lists unlawful behaviors of this type (e.g., incest, adultery, homosexuality, bestiality). As he demonstrated by sending the flood, the judgment on Sodom and Gomorrah, and various judgments on the Israelites, God will judge people who practice these behaviors.

Day Three | God's Amazing Forgiveness

The Very Words of God

> *"I will cleanse you from all your impurities and from all your idols. I will give you a new heart and put a new spirit in you; I will remove from you your heart of stone and give you a heart of flesh. And I will put my Spirit in you and move you to follow my decrees and be careful to keep my laws."*
>
> **Ezekiel 36:25–27**

Bible Discovery

The People God Can Use

Throughout history, God has used people to be his hands and feet in fulfilling his purposes and plans. Sometimes these willing and faithful servants came from surprisingly sinful pasts. Yet they chose faith in God above all else and went on to become influential and powerful witnesses of God in their world.

1. Look up each of the following passages and summarize what you discover about a few people God has used to carry out his amazing plans and purposes in his world:

    Tamar (Genesis 38:6 – 19, 24 – 26)

    Rahab (Joshua 2:1 – 15; 6:22 – 25)

    Ruth (Ruth 1:1 – 8, 14 – 17, 22)

    Bathsheba, the wife of Uriah (2 Samuel 11:1 – 5, 14 – 17, 26 – 27)

2. In light of their life stories, what is significant about how God chose to honor these women generations later? (See Matthew 1:1 – 6.)

3. What do their stories reveal about God's character? His forgiveness? His ability to use anyone who is committed to obeying him in all things?

Reflection

All of us have aspects of our past that we know were contrary to God's will. If you are a Christian, consider the forgiveness you've received from God. What is encouraging to you about the fact that God uses people — in spite of their sinful pasts — to display his glory?

How might the illustrations of God's redemptive work in people's lives that you have explored in this session influence how you view yourself and how you approach your future with God?

As you go about your daily activities, how might you exercise the same faith demonstrated by the people you have just studied?

Take a moment to thank God for using you for his honor in spite of your past, and ask him to use you to show others that he is God.

Memorize

Praise the Lord, O my soul, and forget not all his benefits — who forgives all your sins ... who redeems your life from the pit and crowns you with love and compassion.

Psalm 103:2 – 4

Day Four | Practicing the Principle of First Fruits

The Very Words of God

Honor the LORD with your wealth, with the firstfruits of all your crops; then your barns will be filled to overflowing, and your vats will brim over with new wine.

Proverbs 3:9 – 10

Bible Discovery

Honoring God with Your First Fruits

The principle of "first fruits" reinforces the truth that God is the giver of everything. To give him the first fruits is an act of faith that expresses trust in God to provide the rest. Conversely, to take the first fruits for ourselves is to deny God's ownership of our blessings and to fail to live by faith.

1. According to Deuteronomy 26:1 – 15, what was God's desire concerning the first portion of whatever blessings he gave to Israel?

2. The Word of God is filled with praises and testimonies given in response to God's generous provision for his people. Read Psalms 84:11 – 12; 116:12 – 14; 147:11 and consider the kind of relationship that God desires to have with his people. What roles do God's provision for us and our obedience and trust in him play in that relationship?

3. How did the first fruits principle apply to the spoils of Jer-
    icho, the first city God gave the Israelites in their new land?
    (See Joshua 6:17, 19, 24, 26.)

For what future need did the Israelites indicate they were
depending on God to provide when they gave the first fruits
of the city of Jericho to him?

Reflection

By giving back to God the first portion of what he has provided for
us, we acknowledge him as the source of our provision. We are also
expressing ongoing trust that he will continue to bless us.

What do you think the practice of first fruits does for us and our
relationship with God?

What message do you think this practice sends to a watching
world?

How would you — as a Christian to whom God has given time, talent, and treasure — practice the first fruits principle in your life? Be specific.

Consider the ways in which you are tempted to deny God's role in providing for you by holding back your first fruits (failing to keep the Sabbath, not giving God credit for your blessings, etc.). Take time to pray and reassess God's provision for you and your response to him.

Memorize

How great is your goodness, which you have stored up for those who fear you, which you bestow in the sight of men on those who take refuge in you.

Psalm 31:19

Day Five | Set Apart for God

The Very Words of God

Bring the best of the firstfruits of your soil to the house of the LORD your God.

Exodus 23:19

Bible Discovery

Whatever We Set Apart Is God's — and God's Alone

If we give ourselves to God as his holy people, set apart for him, he will take care of the rest. But if we use what has been set apart for

God to benefit ourselves, we break the first fruits principle. God does not provide for us so that we can honor ourselves but so that we can honor him. When we take for ourselves what belongs to God, we face serious consequences.

1. On God's command, the Israelites went in as God commanded and conquered Jericho. (See Joshua 6:17 – 21, 24.) What did they take for themselves, and what did they devote to God?

    In what way was this a demonstration that the first fruits of their labor belonged to God?

2. Instead of obeying God and giving him the first fruits of Canaan's wealth, what did one Israelite do? (See Joshua 7:1 – 13, 16 – 26.)

    What happened as a consequence to Israel? To Achan and all that he had?

What do you think God's punishment of Achan communicated to the people of Israel? What does it communicate to you?

3. Achan was not the only person to claim for himself what had been given to God at Jericho. The ruins of Jericho were devoted to God as a permanent reminder of God's greatness and faithfulness to his people. No one was to rebuild it (Joshua 6:26), but read 1 Kings 16:29–34 to find out what happened during the reign of King Ahab.

    a. What was King Ahab's attitude toward God and what belonged to him?

    b. What did Hiel of Bethel do, and what price did he pay?

    c. How much of an impact do you think Hiel's action and its consequences had on the people of Israel?

DID YOU REALIZE?
Jericho's Ruins Were Like a Mezuzah

What is a *mezuzah*? It is a small container that holds a rolled parchment inscribed with Bible verses (the text of Deuteronomy 4:4 – 9; 11:13 – 21) that is attached to the doorpost of every religious Jewish home. A Jewish person entering the home touches the *mezuzah* and then kisses his or her fingers as an expression of devotion to the verses it contains. Jewish scholars base the custom of the *mezuzah* on Deuteronomy 6:6, 9: "These commandments that I give you today are to be upon your hearts.... Write them on the door-frames of your houses and on your gates."

The physical presence of a copy of the Deuteronomy commandments provides an excellent reminder of God's desires for his people. In a sense, the ruins of Jericho were also like a *mezuzah*. The mountain pass guarded by Jericho was the main gateway (or doorway, if you will) to the Promised Land from the east. So it was appropriate for God to leave the city's ruins as a testimony, like a *mezuzah*, that the land belonged to him and that his people who lived in it sought to serve him. God wanted his mark of ownership to remain on the land as a reminder that its inhabitants must live by his laws.

Reflection

Do you realize that those who follow Jesus are also a first fruit? James reminded his readers, "Every good and perfect gift is from above, coming down from the Father," then went on to describe believers as those who have been born "through the word of truth, that we might be a kind of firstfruits of all he created" (James 1:17 – 18).

> If you are a Christian, what does it mean to you that you are a first fruit, devoted to God's service?

What has God provided for you — in terms of talent, occupation, financial resources — to use in his service?

Are there any way(s) in which you might be taking back God's first fruits? If so, how much thought have you given to the possible consequences?

What more can you do to honor God for what he provides and to testify to the world that you belong to him?

CONFRONTING EVIL

During the time of the judges in Israel, the Philistines lived on the coastal plain by the Mediterranean Sea. The Israelites, who were far less advanced than the Philistines, lived in the *Shephelah* (the low foothills) and the Judea Mountains to the east. Several broad valleys extend up from the coastal plain through the Shephelah and some distance into the mountains. These valleys became strategic avenues of commerce and culture, linking the coastal plain to the mountains. Trade routes accessed the mountain passes through these valleys, and there were many clashes in the valleys between the opposing cultures of the Philistines and Israelites as each sought to dominate this strategic region.

Beth Shemesh was one of several cities in the valleys that extended into the Shephelah. It stood like a guardhouse over the Sorek Valley, where Philistines and Israelites often fought fiercely. God had given this region of the Shephelah and part of the coastal plain to the small tribe of Dan as its inheritance. However, the tribe of Dan never drove out the Philistines, which created serious problems for God's people.

The Philistines were powerful and their culture was highly sophisticated, but their worship practices were immoral and abhorrent to God. The Philistines worshiped such fertility gods as Dagon, the god of grain; his mistress Ashtoreth, who was associated with war and fertility; and Baal-Zebul, thought to be the son of Dagon. The Israelites were attracted to the Philistines' superior technology, lifestyle, and culture (including worship of their gods), and gradually drew away from God. As punishment, God "delivered them into the hands of the Philistines for forty years" (Judges 13:1).

But God didn't abandon his people. He sent an angel to a childless couple from the tribe of Dan and said, in effect, "You're going to have a child. Now see to it that he becomes a Nazirite." A Nazirite was set apart from his culture. He didn't drink wine, the common drink. Unlike everyone else, he didn't cut his hair. He didn't touch anything dead, so he didn't eat meat. His unique lifestyle was an example and reminder to God's people of what it meant to be set apart for God, to be different from the surrounding, ungodly culture.

After God's Spirit stirred inside him, the couple's son, Samson, began confronting the evil Philistine culture. He used foxes to burn up huge wheat fields, carried the city gates of Gaza about forty-five miles to Hebron, and killed many Philistine soldiers. As long as he remained dedicated to God's values, Samson effectively accomplished what God had called him to do. As time passed, however, Samson compromised more and more with the Philistines' value system. Consequently he lost spiritual and physical power, rendering his walk with God and his mission ineffective.

Samson was not the only Israelite who was unwilling to confront the Philistine culture as God had instructed. As a whole, the Israelites had failed to live out their distinctiveness, and when the Philistines began invading their turf in the mountains, the Israelites realized they were in serious trouble. In a last-ditch effort to regain God's power, Eli — the high priest — sent the ark of the covenant into battle. The Philistines captured the ark, but it brought them such great trouble that they returned it (along with gifts of gold) to the Israelites. Rejoicing greatly, the Israelites offered a sacrifice to God and left a standing stone to mark the spot where God's presence had been returned to them.

Opening Thoughts (4 minutes)

The Very Words of God

> "You must not live according to the customs of the nations I am going to drive out before you…. I said to you, 'You will possess their land; I will give it to you as an inheritance, a land flowing with milk and honey.' I am the LORD your God, who has set you apart from the nations."
>
> *Leviticus 20:23 – 24*

Think About It

God has always made it clear that the values and lifestyles of the world — whether it be our world or the world of the ancient Israelites — are sinful. He also makes it clear that his people are to confront the values of the world by serving him and choosing to live according to his values. Yet the values and lifestyle of the world still attract us and tug at our hearts.

In which areas of our lives do you think we are vulnerable to compromising our commitment to live for God and to obey him in all things? What are the consequences of even "small" compromises?

DVD Teaching Notes (28 minutes)

Beth Shemesh: focal point of conflict in the Shephelah

The Philistines—the people, land, culture, technology

The importance of fulfilling God's calling

Samson—set apart for God

The cost of compromise

DVD Discussion (6 minutes)

1. Take a moment to study the map on page 101. Notice where the cities of the Shephelah are located in relationship to the valleys linking the mountains to the coastal plain. Why did cities adjacent to these valleys, such as Beth Shemesh, play such a strategic role in the life and history of Israel?

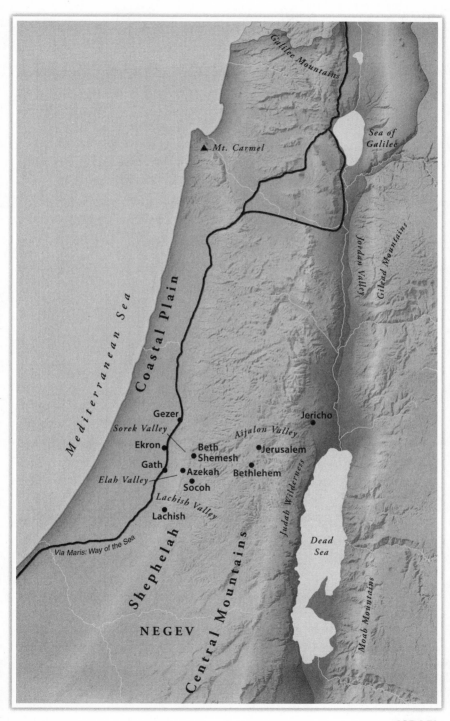

ISRAEL

THINK ABOUT IT
Why Beth Shemesh?

- Guarded a passage between the coastal plain (Philistine territory) and the mountains of Judah (Israelite territory).
- Was founded during the early Bronze Age — nearly five thousand years ago.
- Was destroyed and later rebuilt at least six times — once by the Babylonians on their way to destroy Jerusalem for the first time (588 – 587 BC).
- Contained many olive oil and fabric dying installations and wheat production industries during King David's time.

**THE FERTILE SOREQ VALLEY
AS SEEN FROM BETH SHEMESH**

2. What did you learn that was new to you about the Philistines and their culture? How does this help you understand the significance of what took place between the Israelites and the Philistines?

3. In what ways did Samson compromise his calling to live for God as a Nazirite? What were the results?

THE MAKING OF A CITY

The environment of the Middle East, including Israel, is harsh and mostly unsuitable for settlement. For a location such as Beth Shemesh to be habitable, three conditions were needed:

Fresh Water

Although rainfall is plentiful in some regions of Israel, most rain falls during the winter. Many ancient communities stored rainwater in cisterns. If a season received below-average rainfall, cisterns dried up and people abandoned their city. If an enemy laid siege to the city, only cisterns inside the city walls were available, so when the water ran out the city fell. Jerusalem was built next to the spring of Gihon. Meggido, Hazor, and Gezer reached fresh water through tunnels dug through bedrock.

Profitable Occupation

People needed the opportunity to grow a consistent food supply or be able to buy food.

- Olive trees flourished in Judea and Galilee.
- Wheat grew in the valleys of Judea and Jezreel.
- Shepherds raised sheep and goats in the wilderness.
- Chorazin (Israel) and Ekron (Philistine) had large facilities for processing olive oil.
- Jerusalem was famous for its purple dye.
- Some cities provided supplies to travelers on the Via Maris, the major trade route.

A Defensible Location

The political climate in the ancient Near East was volatile, so cities were typically built on hills surrounding fertile valleys so inhabitants could defend themselves better.

Small Group Bible Discovery and Discussion (13 minutes)

The Strategic Shephelah

The foothills of Israel — the Shephelah — served as a buffer zone between the mountains where most of the Israelites lived and the Philistine cities on the coastal plain. Because control of the Shephelah ensured the security and power of the dominant culture, many battles between the Philistines and Israelites took place there. Although the Israelites failed to drive the Philistines out of the Promised Land, God periodically raised up heroes to confront the Philistines in the Shephelah. These heroes also reminded Israel of what God had called his people to accomplish.

1. First Samuel describes many of the encounters between the Israelites and the Philistines that took place in the Shephelah. As you read highlights from just a few of those accounts, discuss the location and circumstances, who God raised up to stand for him, what the odds appeared to be, and the results.

   1 Samuel 7:7 - 14

   1 Samuel 13:5 - 7, 16 - 18

1 Samuel 14:1, 8 – 16, 22 – 23

1 Samuel 17:1 – 3, 8 – 9, 34 – 36

2. Israel was certainly on the "front lines" in the territorial con-
    frontations with the Philistines, yet it was difficult for the
    Israelites to avoid assimilating the values of the Philistine cul-
    ture, so their influence for God was compromised. Where do
    you think the confrontation of cultural values takes place in
    our world today? What must we do to avoid compromising
    our values and influence for God?

DID YOU KNOW?
The Shephelah

- Is a twelve-to-fifteen-mile-wide region of foothills in Judea that are located between the coastal plain to the west and the Judea Mountains to the east.
- The valleys of the Shephelah functioned as corridors between the mountains and the coastal plain.
- The place where the Israelites interacted (peacefully or not) with the Philistines. Most Philistine-Israelite conflicts occurred here.
- Symbolizes for us the places where God's values meet the pagan practices of Western culture. Like the Israelites, we have a crucial choice: to withdraw to the "mountains" or to be on the front lines, confronting the secular values of our world and with God's blessing seeking to gain control of the "coastal plain" in our neighborhoods, cities, countries, and beyond.

Faith Lesson (3 minutes)

It is not easy to live on the "front lines" of the Shephelah. The visible battles are difficult, but the inner battles of the heart — the battles to stand strong and live according to God's values — are even more challenging.

1. Which aspect(s) of modern culture that often can lead people into sin is attractive to you? Wealth? Pleasure? Gratification? Fame? Be honest.

2. What steps can you take to strengthen your commitment to living out God's values so that you are able to stand firm when you are tempted to compromise in any of these areas?

Closing (1 minute)

Read the following verses aloud. Then pray together, asking God to give you a passionate commitment to stand firm for him and influence culture without compromise. Invite God to reveal to you any area(s) of your lives in which you are compromising — in thought, word, or action.

Memorize

> *Do not love the world or anything in the world. If anyone loves the world, the love of the Father is not in him. For everything in the world — the cravings of sinful man, the lust of his eyes and the boasting of what he has and does — comes not from the Father but from the world. The world and its desires pass away, but the man who does the will of God lives forever.*
>
> **1 John 2:15 – 17**

SPOTLIGHT ON THE EVIDENCE
The Making of a Tel

Israel is dotted with distinctive hills called *tels* that are characterized by steep sides and flat tops. (*Tel* is the Hebrew spelling that we use in this study; *tell* is the English spelling.) These hills comprise multiple layers of ancient settlements, each of which was built on the ruins of a previous settlement. In general terms, here's how tels, including Tel Beth Shemesh, were formed.

- **Stage 1:** People settled on the site, eventually building a wall and gate. Often they built a rampart against the wall to protect the hill from erosion and keep enemies away from the base of the wall.
- **Stage 2:** Inhabitants abandoned the settlement due to war, drought, or other calamity. The ruins faded into the landscape.
- **Stage 3:** People moved back to the same site, filled in holes, gathered larger building stones, leveled off the hill, and rebuilt. Then the city's success attracted enemies ... and the cycle of destruction and rebuilding continued.

continued on next page . . .

- **Stage 4:** Layers upon layers of ruins accumulated (sort of like a layer cake) so the hill became higher. Each layer—or stratum—records what life was like during a particular time. Artifacts discovered in the tel reveal a great deal about how people lived during specific time periods.

Tels help us understand more clearly the Bible's message by providing relevant information about life during biblical times. Each tel is, in effect, a unique gift from God to help us better understand his Word.

DIAGRAM OF A TEL

Making God Known to the World

In-Depth Personal Study Sessions

Day One │ Who Were the Philistines?

The Very Words of God

> *I will establish your borders from the Red Sea to the Sea of the Philistines,*
> *and from the desert to the River. I will hand over to you the people who live*
> *in the land and you will drive them out before you.... Do not let them live in*
> *your land, or they will cause you to sin against me, because the worship of*
> *their gods will certainly be a snare to you.*
>
> > *Exodus 23:31 – 33*

Bible Discovery

The Philistines Test Israel

About 1100 BC, a group of people, the Philistines, migrated from the
Aegean world, from the area we know as Greece, and settled along
the Mediterranean coast of present-day Israel. Also known as "people
of the sea," the Philistines established a series of city states and
developed a highly sophisticated culture. They had the technology
to make and use iron and established a thriving olive oil trade. They
were very active in their worship of fertility gods. As the Old Testament records, the Philistines engaged Israel in a long-term power
struggle for domination of the Shephelah, the political and commer-
cial landscape, and the culture itself.

1. What do the following passages reveal about the Philistines,
   their culture, and their relationship with Israel?

   Judges 1:17 – 19, 27 – 2:3

1 Samuel 4:5 – 9

1 Samuel 13:19 – 22

1 Samuel 31:1 – 13

1 Kings 22:51 – 53; 2 Kings 1:1 – 4

2. What role did God allow the Philistines (and other nations)
   to play in the Israelites' lives and why? (See Judges 2:20 – 3:4;
   2 Chronicles 28:17 – 19.)

DATA FILE
The Philistines
History
Sailed from the Aegean world (Greece) and settled along the eastern shores of the Mediterranean Sea around 1100 BC, about the time the Israelites entered the Promised Land from the east. Developed a sophisticated culture and established city states.

Location
All five key Philistine cities were located near the Via Maris trade route, which went through the coastal plain. Consequently Philistines dominated world trade and greatly influenced other nations.

Industry
Developed an elaborate olive pressing industry. (At Ekron alone, about two hundred installations produced olive oil — perhaps more than a thousand tons per year.) Also famous for iron making, a skill Israel had not yet learned.

Military Might
Philistine soldiers were quite tall, clean shaven, and wore breastplates and small kilts. Soldiers carried small shields and fought with straight swords and spears.

Artistic Skill
Created gracefully shaped pottery with intricate red-and-black geometric designs on white backgrounds.

Religion
Very sophisticated and immoral. Built carefully planned temples in Gaza, Ashdod, and Beth Shean. Dagon, their main god, was thought to be the god of grain. The goddess Ashtoreth, believed to be his mistress, was associated with war and fertility. Baal-Zebul, thought to be Dagon's son, was worshiped at Ekron. The worship of this deity involved sacred prostitution and possibly child sacrifice. By New Testament times, the name Beelzebub — long used to describe the most evil and perverted practices and people of the ancient Near East — had become a synonym for the Devil (Matthew 10:25; 12:24).

Reflection

We all have a tendency to become lax in our commitment to obey God and to live in such a way that others know he is God. Proverbs 3:11 – 12 gives us a picture of how God teaches those he loves to obey him: "My son, do not despise the LORD's discipline and do not resent his rebuke, because the LORD disciplines those he loves, as a father the son he delights in."

How does this perspective help you understand why God allowed various pagan nations such as the Philistines to come into power and "test" the Israelites who had disobeyed him repeatedly?

What kind of relationship did God desire to have with the Israelites, and what impact did God's "discipline" have on them?

What kinds of challenges have you faced (or may you be facing) that tested your desire and commitment to live according to God's values in your culture? What have those challenges accomplished in your life and in your relationship with God?

Day Two | Set Apart to Live for God

The Very Words of God

> *Know that the LORD has set apart the godly for himself.*
>
> **Psalm 4:3**

Bible Discovery

Samson: Set Apart for God

You probably know the story of Samson — his amazing feats of strength; his relationship with Delilah, who betrayed him; and his final act of destruction against the Philistines. But there's more to the story, and it has to do with Samson being set apart by God as a Nazirite. To be a Nazirite was to be different, to stand out from the crowd. A Nazirite was a living visual aid who reminded the Israelites of their need to separate themselves from sin and the pagan culture around them.

1. In what ways was Samson different even before he was born? Who had set him apart for God, and what was he to do? (See Judges 13:1 - 5.)

2. Read Numbers 6:1 - 12, 21. What do the following verses say about what was required to be a Nazirite?

Numbers 6	Requirements to Be a Nazirite
vv. 1 – 3	
v. 4	
v. 5	
vv. 6 – 7	
v. 8	
vv. 9 – 12	
v. 21	

3. In order to accomplish all that God had called him to do,
    what did Samson need from God? (See Judges 13:25.)

Reflection

As Christians, we too have been set apart by God to accomplish his
purposes:"For we are God's workmanship, created in Christ Jesus to
do good works, which God prepared in advance for us to do" (Ephesians 2:10).

If you were to (1) take seriously your commitment to obey God
and place all aspects of your life under the dominion of his value
system and (2) apply the same kind of dedication to living out
your personal mission as the Nazirites applied to their vows,
how would your life be different?

In what ways would you stand out?

What would people see in you that they may not see now?

What role does the Holy Spirit play as you seek to live out your life commitment to God?

Memorize

In your hearts set apart Christ as Lord.

1 Peter 3:15

Day Three | Impacting Culture for God

The Very Words of God

Summon your power, O God; show us your strength, O God, as you have done before.

Psalm 68:28

Bible Discovery

Confrontation and Compromise: A Struggle for Dominance

Samson offers us a challenging look at the fine line between cultural confrontation and cultural compromise. God had made him a Nazirite and set him apart so that he could effectively confront the Philistines and deliver Israel. Yet over time Samson made compromises with the Philistine culture that led to dire consequences for him and for Israel.

1. Read Judges 14:1 – 4; 15:1 – 5, 9 – 15 to discover how Samson sought opportunities to confront the Philistines.

   a. What actions did Samson take in these encounters?

    b.   How much of an impact did his actions have on the Philistines?

    c.   What kind of impact do you think Samson's actions had on the Israelites? (See Judges 15:20.)

2.   Read the following verses to discover in what ways Samson violated his Nazirite vow and compromised his calling:

    Numbers 6:6 – 7; Judges 14:5 – 9

    Numbers 6:4; Judges 14:10 (Note: the word translated "feast" means "drinking bout.")

    Judges 16:1 – 3

3.   When Samson lived a lifestyle that was completely devoted to God's values, he was effective. When he compromised that value system, what happened? (See Judges 16:4, 15 – 21.)

Reflection

As God's people we, like Samson, are called to live on the front lines where opposing values clash and actively influence the world for God. But we can live out a God-centered lifestyle and confront ungodliness only when we refuse to adopt ungodly values. That is why the warning of 1 John 2:15 is so important for us to remember: "Do not love the world or anything in the world. If anyone loves the world, the love of the Father is not in him." We must be very careful to remain distinct from the world's culture, not to compromise with it.

In what ways might you be trying to avoid the battles of living for God instead of "living in the Shephelah," the place where God's values meet the values of your culture?

Which aspects of your culture do you believe God would have you confront? In what ways might you be prone to compromise if you do so?

In your everyday activities, what are the implications of choosing to love God and not the world?

Which area(s) of your life have you not completely and distinctively committed to God?

In what ways has this compromise affected your witness and weakened your impact for God?

What are you going to do about it?

Day Four | Our Sovereign God at Work

The Very Words of God

"I am God, and there is no other; I am God, and there is none like me. I make known the end from the beginning, from ancient times, what is still to come. I say: My purpose will stand, and I will do all that I please....What I have said, that will I bring about; what I have planned, that will I do."

Isaiah 46:9 – 11

Bible Discovery

God Accomplishes His Work Even through Our Failures

Samson's failure to live out his calling by confronting the culture of the Philistines and displaying God's greatness and holiness to a watching world is essentially Israel's greatest failure as well. Samson failed to live out his calling when he began to participate in the value system of the culture he was supposed to confront. For generations before him, and for generations after him, Israel did the same thing. Yet God can use even the greatest failures of his people to accomplish his purposes. Just as God faithfully continued to work through the flaws and failures of his people in ancient Israel, he does the same for us today.

1. One way that Samson compromised his calling was by his relationship with Delilah, a Philistine woman living in the Sorek Valley.

    a. What were the short-term and long-term consequences of Samson's failure in this area?

Immediate Consequences (Judg. 16:5, 16–21)	Longer-term Consequences (Judg. 16:23–30)

    b. In light of the lusty willfulness Samson displayed during a portion of his life, what change in attitude is evident in his final prayer to God? What resulted?

    c. As you consider all that happened in Samson's life and what God had intended Samson's life to be, what do you learn about God's faithfulness and power in accomplishing his purposes?

2. Clearly God can accomplish his sovereign purposes despite the disobedience, failures, or weaknesses of his people. He has done it over and over again. Consider, for example, these events that took place in the valley near Beth Shemesh:

   a. Israel was fighting the Philistines and losing badly. What did Israel do to try to salvage their situation, and what was the result? (See 1 Samuel 4:2 - 11.)

   b. What happened among the Philistines while they had possession of the ark of the covenant? What message was God sending to the Philistines without the help of his people? (See 1 Samuel 5:1 - 6:2.)

   c. Where and how did the Philistines return the ark of the covenant to Israel? What sign were they watching for, and what did it mean to them? (See 1 Samuel 6:7 - 12.)

   d. What did the return of the ark mean to the people of Israel? How did they respond immediately? In the long term? What did they learn about their commitment to serving God? (See 1 Samuel 6:13 - 7:4.)

Reflection

Our failure to fulfill the work to which God calls us certainly has serious consequences. But when we are weak and even when we fail, our sovereign God makes himself known. He is faithful to accomplish his purposes because his "power is made perfect in weakness."

> Consider times when God has used your weakness or the weaknesses of others to demonstrate his strength and/or accomplish his will. In what ways does God's commitment and faithfulness to accomplish his plan in these situations give you hope when you feel overwhelmed or discouraged?

> When you feel inadequate to face a difficult challenge, to what extent does your knowledge of God's character affect your willingness to obey his calling and trust him to produce the results?

Day Five | Called to Be Different

The Very Words of God

> *"I have revealed and saved and proclaimed — I, and not some foreign god among you. You are my witnesses," declares the LORD, "that I am God."*

Isaiah 43:12

Bible Discovery

Taking a Stand That Makes an Impact

From the beginning, God has called his people to an important mission: "You are my witnesses ... that I am God" (Isaiah 43:12). He placed the Israelites at the crossroads of the ancient world so that through them the world would know that he — Yahweh — is the one true God. But danger lurked in the Israelites' mission. The very world into which they were to bring the "culture of God" had a seductive culture of its own, and Israel often succumbed to its appeal. At certain times, however, the people of Israel took a stand — sometimes at their peril — to influence their culture and their world for God.

In each of the following situations, how did God use his people to make an impact for his kingdom? What was the result?

Scripture Text	What Happened	Impact on the Culture
Judg. 6:24–32		
2 Kings 22:1–23:25		
2 Chron. 22:1–23:3; 23:11–21		
2 Kings 18:1–8, 17, 28–36; 19:9–19, 35–36		
Judg. 4:1–10, 13–24		

Reflection

Throughout this study, you have explored the challenges God's people faced as they sought to fulfill their calling to live God-centered, God-honoring lives in the midst of cultures that did not honor him. Take a few moments now to translate what you have learned about the world of ancient Israel into the culture and value systems of the world in which you live.

1. Identify the opposing cultures or values:

    "The Philistines of today (the _____)
    express their values by (in) _____
    _____. The Israelites of today (the _____
    _____) express their values by
    (in) _____."

    Where do you see the values of each group expressed most clearly?

2. Identify where these cultures or value systems meet:

    "The Shephelah of our lives is _____
    _____."

3. Identify the culture or value system that has the most power and control to influence the world:

    "The coastal plain of today is _____
    _____, and it is controlled mainly by the _____
    _____ value system."

4. As you did this exercise, what did you learn that will influ-
    ence how you live out your calling to show the world that
    God is the one true God?

Memorize

*"I have revealed and saved and proclaimed — I, and not some foreign god
among you. You are my witnesses," declares the* LORD, *"that I am God."*

Isaiah 43:12

IRON OF CULTURE

This session was filmed at Tel Azekah, a five-acre site overlooking the Valley of Elah. Tel Azekah stands as a reminder that defending the Shephelah — the foothills between the coastal plains where the Philistines lived and the mountains where most of the Israelites lived — was critical to Israel's survival. Azekah guarded an important gateway into the mountains that provided access to Bethlehem (only twelve miles from Azekah) and to Jerusalem (a few miles north of Bethlehem). No wonder the Philistines and other pagan cultures wanted to capture and hold Azekah!

We will focus our attention on the battle between the Philistines and Israelites in the Valley of Elah during the reign of King Saul. Imagine the scene. Both armies face each other. For forty days Goliath, a hardened Philistine warrior more than nine feet tall, taunts the Israelite army and ridicules their God. Then a young shepherd named David, who is perhaps ten or twelve years old, arrives from Bethlehem to bring food to his brothers, who are there to fight for Israel. Appalled by the insults Goliath hurls at the God of Israel, David is compelled by God's Spirit to fight the giant.

Humanly speaking, David has little to offer. He has no sword or spear. King Saul's armor doesn't fit him. So David carries nothing into battle but a powerful faith in God and expertise with his sling.

Goliath, on the other hand, is equipped with the latest weapons: a sword, javelin, and iron-tipped spear. His suit of armor weighs 125 pounds. Goliath represents more than a formidable military challenge: he represents what is evil and opposed to God. David recognizes the true nature of Goliath's challenge and accepts it with the right motive — so that the world would "know that there is a God in Israel."

The cultural implications of the battle between David and Goliath are worth noting. The Philistines were masters at making and using iron and most likely introduced iron making into the ancient Near East. Because of their technological superiority, the Philistines dominated not only in warfare but in material prosperity and commerce. In contrast, the Israelites didn't know how to work with iron. They even had to go to the Philistines to have their tools sharpened (1 Samuel 13:19 – 21). On the battlefield in the Valley of Elah, only two Israelites — King Saul and his son, Jonathan — possessed a sword or spear (1 Samuel 13:22). No wonder the Israelites were afraid!

After David's stone knocked Goliath to the ground, David drew Goliath's sword and cut off the giant's head. It was a great victory for Israel. In time, however, King Saul became jealous of David's victories and tried to kill him.

David, his men, and their families fled to Achish — son of the Philistine king of Gath (1 Samuel 27) — who gave David the Philistine city of Ziklag. Some scholars believe that while living in Gath David or one of his men discovered the Philistines' secret of iron technology and brought it to the Israelites. However it occurred, the Israelites learned to work with iron at about the time David became king of Israel. Consequently, the Philistines lost power and influence as Israel became the dominant culture in the region (2 Samuel 5:17 – 25).

Opening Thoughts (4 minutes)

The Very Words of God

> Let them know that you, whose name is the LORD — that you alone are the Most High over all the earth.

> **Psalm 83:18**

Think About It

When you face difficult — or let's face it, "impossible" — situations in which you are outnumbered, ill equipped, outmaneuvered, and under trained, how do you respond?

When you feel overwhelmed, what does it take for you to keep pursuing the goal ahead? What motivates you to regroup and refocus your efforts on the task at hand?

DVD Teaching Notes (20 minutes)

Azekah: guardian of the Judea Mountains

Goliath—champion of the Philistines

David—shepherd from Bethlehem

The "iron" of culture

Key to the battle

DVD Discussion (7 minutes)

1. On the map of Israel on page 129, note the locations of
    Azekah, Socoh, and the Valley of Elah. Note how far into the
    Shephelah Azekah is located.

    For what reasons was the confrontation between David and
    Goliath in the Valley of Elah critical to the survival of Israel?

    What do you think was at stake politically, culturally, and
    spiritually?

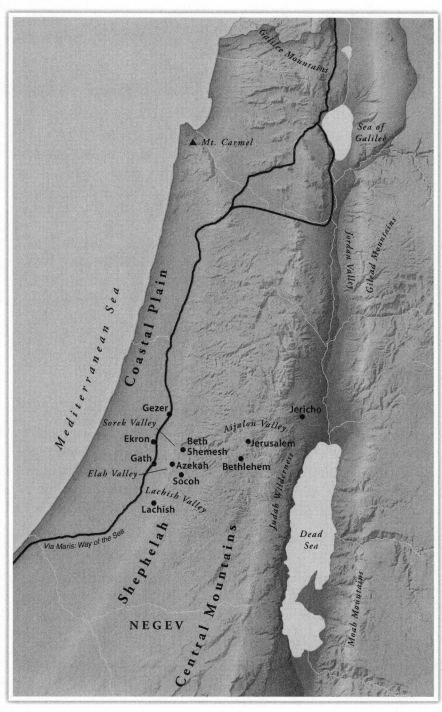

ISRAEL

DATA FILE
Metalworking Technology and Power in the
Ancient Near East

Before 1200 BC, bronze—a combination of copper and tin—was the metal of choice for people of the ancient Near East. Perhaps this was because the melting point of copper is 1,100 degrees Celsius and the melting point of iron is 1,550 degrees Celsius. Although bronze was a significant technological step beyond stone and wood, it was soft and didn't hold an edge well. Then numerous invasions (the Philistines and Israelites entered Canaan at this time), wars, and collapses of cultures resulted in a shortage of tin, which led to a scarcity of bronze. The time was right for a new technology.

During the thirteenth century BC, an Aegean people—the Philistines—migrated to the ancient Near East. Although they may not have invented iron-making technology, they used it effectively. In fact, they developed a process that included leaving iron in the fire long enough to absorb the carbon from firewood to form a more malleable form of iron—steel. This superior metal so revolutionized the world that it gave its name to the next six hundred years of human history—the Iron Age.

As a technological advancement during biblical times, iron could be compared to nuclear energy or the most advanced computers today. Iron revolutionized how people lived—how much land they could plow, how much stone they could shape, how much wood they could cut. It greatly changed warfare, just as gunpowder did centuries later. In fact, iron determined which cultures would dominate world events.

For many years, the Philistines kept their iron technology secret so others could not use it. Since the Philistines lived on the coastal plain along the international trade routes, they had great access and influence throughout the world of the ancient Near East. Thus, the Philistine culture dominated the region during the early Iron Age, much as Western nations shape the cultures of developing nations today.

Between the time David killed Goliath and when he became king of Israel (2 Samuel 5), however, the Israelites learned the secret of iron technology. So they became the dominant culture in the region — until they were unfaithful to God. Iron technology was one of the means by which God blessed David and provided a people, nation, and kingly pattern for the coming Son of David — the Messiah.

2. Goliath taunted the army of Israel for forty days, yet not one man stepped forward to fight. For what reasons were the men of Israel afraid to fight?

3. What finally enabled the Israelites to gain power and influence over the Philistines?

Small Group Bible Discovery and Discussion (18 minutes)

Equipped for Battle?

When we seek to accomplish God's work, our motivation to pursue righteousness and our faith in God are far more significant than our talents or our resources. You see, God qualifies and gifts each of us to reveal his greatness to a watching world. No matter how inadequate our resources and experience may appear to be from a human perspective, we don't have to be anything other than the people God has created us to be in order to influence our culture for him. Who he has made us to be is enough!

1. As the Israelite and Philistine armies faced one another in the Valley of Elah, the great disparity in the quality of their military equipment was evident. Read the following references and write down the military equipment available to each party.

Scripture Text	Philistines/Goliath	Israelites/David
1 Sam. 13:5, 19, 22		
1 Sam. 17:4–7, 38–43		

Note: Although not mentioned in these passages, the Israelites and Philistines both used bows and arrows in battle. (Israelite arrows were about eighteen inches long and could travel fifty to seventy feet.) The Philistines also could have used their iron chariots in the wide Valley of Elah.

SPOTLIGHT ON THE EVIDENCE

After finding carvings of Philistine soldiers in the temple of Ramses III in Egypt, archaeologists discovered that the soldiers:

- Wore feathered helmets secured under the chin by a leather strap. Headbands, probably made of metal, held the feathers in place.
- Wore breastplates and short skirts that had wide hems and tassels.
- Were clean shaven and quite tall.
- Sometimes carried small, round shields and straight swords.

2. In David's mind, what was really at stake in the contest between Israel and Goliath? (See 1 Samuel 17:26, 45.)

3. David's response to Goliath's verbal attack provides great insight into David's faith in God and his understanding of the nature of the battle with Goliath. (See 1 Samuel 17:45 – 47.)

    a. What, from David's perspective, was the battle about?

    b. What, then, would be the outcome?

4. What do you think God wanted to demonstrate by choosing David — a young shepherd armed with a sling — to fight Goliath?

    What conclusion(s) can we draw from this story about the way in which God uses people — and their most basic talents and simple tools — to accomplish his purposes?

Faith Lesson (5 minutes)

David used the tools of his culture in the way God had gifted him to show "that there is a God in Israel." He triumphed because he acted for the right reason; he placed his trust in God; and God honored his faith. Each of us has the same challenge: whether or not to step out in faith to use the gifts and talents God has given us to show that God is God.

1. How might David's motives for challenging Goliath apply to you, whom God also has called to challenge the evils of your culture?

2. In what ways does the fact that God gifted David to use the tools of his culture to show that there is a God in Israel empower you to use your gifts and talents to accomplish God's purposes?

3. Which of your talents, no matter how insignificant they may seem from a human viewpoint, might God want to use for his purposes? Which of them are you willing to use in his service?

Closing (1 minute)

Many, many times in the history of Israel, God accomplished a mighty work to rescue his people from evil and preserve the honor of his name. Read the following verse aloud, then pray about what you have learned during this session. Ask God to empower you to challenge the evils of your culture, using whichever gifts and/or abilities he has given to you.

Memorize

The LORD your God, who is among you, is a great and awesome God.

Deuteronomy 7:21

Making God Known to the World

In-Depth Personal Study Sessions

Day One | More Than a Clash of Cultures

The Very Words of God

> *The eyes of the LORD are on the righteous and his ears are attentive to their cry; the face of the LORD is against those who do evil, to cut off the memory of them from the earth.*
>
> *Psalm 34:15 – 16*

Bible Discovery

Exposing the Real Battle Lines

The battle in the Valley of Elah is significant not just because David, a young shepherd untrained in warfare, defeated a giant of a warrior. It is significant not just because Israel defeated the Philistines. This battle represented something far bigger — the classic spiritual conflict between God and the forces of evil. It is a conflict that continues today.

CULTURES IN CONTRAST

Philistines	Israelites
Lived on the fertile coastal plain	Lived mainly in mountainous areas
Had advanced iron technology	Had primitive technology
Worshiped many gods through extremely immoral religious practices, including sacred prostitution	Worshiped the one true God — the God of Israel

1. The battle scene for control of Azekah and the Valley of Elah is described in 1 Samuel 17:1 – 3.

   a. Where did the two armies position themselves for this battle?

   b. Which army was the aggressor, and why did the people want control of this area?

   c. Why was this battle in the Shephelah so important to the defenders?

2. According to 1 Samuel 17:4 – 7, 51, what kind of warrior was Goliath? How great a foe do you think he would have been against most men? Against those who did and did not have comparable weapons?

FACT FILE
Goliath

- Was a hardened warrior more than nine feet tall.
- Wore a coat of bronze "scale" armor weighing 125 pounds. (The coat of mail was designed to protect its wearer without restricting movement.)
- Carried a spear that had a fifteen-pound point.
- Came from the Philistine city of Gath.
- Wore a bronze javelin on his back and a bronze helmet.
- Defied the God of Israel ... and paid for it with his life.

PHILISTINE ARMOR

3. The description of Goliath in Scripture has caught the attention of some scholars who see it as being more than a mere physical image and, therefore, meaning more than most readers might realize. For example, the description of his armor as "scale" armor is also a description befitting a snake, which represents the Devil in the garden of Eden. Some scholars also point to the ways in which multiples of the number six (in measurements of length, conversion to cubits results in multiples of six), which also represent the Devil, were used to describe Goliath. Reread 1 Samuel 17:4 – 7 with these images in mind. What does this help you understand about the nature of this confrontation between Israel and the Philistines?

4. Who, in effect, did Goliath defy every time he shouted out his challenges? What does this reveal about the nature of the battle? (See 1 Samuel 17:8-10.)

5. How did each side — the Philistines, the Israelites — respond to David's victory? (See 1 Samuel 17:51-53.)

Why is it significant that the Philistines, who had such great military superiority, became so afraid of Israel?

Check the map on page 129 and notice how far the Israelites chased the Philistines. What did this achieve for Israel?

Reflection

Just as the battle between Israel and the Philistines, between David and Goliath, represented far more than a territorial skirmish, the cultural battle between God's people and the values of the world involves far more than lifestyle preferences.

What loud challenges shouted against God's people today are really a defiance of God and his righteous sovereignty?

As David faced Goliath, what did he believe about Goliath, God, and himself that empowered him to act?

As you consider the evil that needs to be confronted in the culture of your world, how do your beliefs about your opponent, God, and yourself empower you (or discourage you) to take action?

Day Two | The Battle between God and Satan

The Very Words of God

> *Our struggle is not against flesh and blood, but against the rulers, against the authorities, against the powers of this dark world and against the spiritual forces of evil in the heavenly realms.*
>
> *Ephesians 6:12*

Bible Discovery

The Great Struggle in Human History

Since Satan's first encounter with Adam and Eve, the battle between God and Satan has been played out countless times in human history. Note the ways in which a few of the writers of Scripture revealed their understanding of this cosmic battle.

1. According to Genesis 3:1 - 6, 14 - 15, what did God say would happen concerning the relationship between human beings and the Devil and his offspring (seed)?

    How would Satan's descendants be destroyed?

    What, then, might be the significance of the way in which Goliath died? (See 1 Samuel 17:48 - 49.)

2. Daniel 3:1 – 6 describes a golden statue that King Nebuchad-
    nezzar built in Babylon for the people of his empire to
    worship.

    a. Note carefully the height and width of the statue in
        cubits, which is how measurements were expressed
        in Aramaic (a cubit is approximately 1.5 feet). If in the
        minds of biblical writers the number six represents
        Satan, what did this statue represent?

    b. Convert the height of Goliath into cubits (1 Samuel 17:4)
        and compare it to the dimensions of this statue. What
        does this reveal about who Goliath represents?

Reflection

The battle against evil that God's people have been called to fight is
not over. That's why the apostle Peter reminds believers to be "self-
controlled and alert" because "your enemy the devil prowls around
… looking for someone to devour" (1 Peter 5:8).

Why is it important that we each understand the reality of the
ongoing spiritual battle between God and Satan — and its real
consequences?

Consider for a moment issues that today cause conflict between
the Christian community and secular society.

Who are the real opponents in this battle?

Have we, as a Christian community, tended to see them as God's battles or our own?

How does this affect our approach to them?

Think about how quickly David perceived the true nature of the battle with Goliath and how quickly he responded with total confidence in God. What can you learn from David about standing firm and trusting God when facing evil?

Read and memorize 1 Peter 5:8 – 11. It tells us how to perceive the battle, what to do, and who has the power. May it encourage you to stand firm for God in the battles he has called you to fight.

Memorize

Be self-controlled and alert. Your enemy the devil prowls around like a roaring lion looking for someone to devour. Resist him, standing firm in the faith, because you know that your brothers throughout the world are undergoing the same kind of sufferings. And the God of all grace, who called you to his eternal glory in Christ, after you have suffered a little while, will himself restore you and make you strong, firm and steadfast. To him be the power for ever and ever. Amen.

1 Peter 5:8 – 11

Day Three | The Far-Reaching Consequences of Disobedience

The Very Words of God

> *Be very careful to keep the commandment and the law that Moses the servant of the LORD gave you: to love the LORD your God, to walk in all his ways, to obey his commands, to hold fast to him and to serve him with all your heart and all your soul.*

> *Joshua 22:5*

Bible Discovery

"A King Like the Other Nations"

Long before Saul was anointed to be Israel's first king, God had warned his people to appoint a king of his choosing who would obey him faithfully (Deuteronomy 17:14-20). But when Israel demanded a king to lead them and fight their battles, they weren't thinking about the king God wanted for them; they were rejecting God in favor of a king like those of the nations around them. Often Israel got just that — a king the world would choose, not one God would choose.

1. Early in the Israelites' history, what had God commanded them to do once they settled in the Promised Land? (See Deuteronomy 25:17-19.)

2. During Saul's reign, God gave him an important task to accomplish. (See 1 Samuel 15:1-29.)

    a. What job did God entrust to Saul? (See 1 Samuel 15:1-3.)

b. In what ways did Saul obey God, and in what ways did Saul disobey? (See 1 Samuel 15:4 – 9.)

c. What was Samuel's response, and how did Saul attempt to justify his actions? (See 1 Samuel 15:13 – 21.)

d. What consequence did Saul and his family face? (See 1 Samuel 15:22 – 29.)

THINK ABOUT IT

About four hundred years after Saul disobeyed God by sparing King Agag, King Xerxes of Persia gave permission to one of his subjects, Haman, to destroy the Jews (Esther 3:1 – 13). Haman was a descendent of King Agag! So King Saul's failure to obey God completely not only cost him his throne, his family, and his life, but four centuries later it jeopardized God's plan of salvation.

God had not forgotten his people, however, nor would he allow his plan of salvation to be thwarted. God had placed a young Jewish woman, Esther, as queen of King Xerxes. She was, in fact, a descendant of Saul's father, and it fell on her shoulders to risk her life to save her people (1 Samuel 9:1 – 2; Esther 2:5 – 7; 4:1 – 8:14). She was faithful to obey God's calling and saved the Jews from the tragedy her ancestor Saul had created.

Do you think Saul ever imagined how great an impact his disobedience would have centuries later? How often do we think of the possible consequences, near term and long term, of our own disobedience?

3. In Deuteronomy 17:14 – 20, God provided clear instructions
    for future kings of his chosen people. A king who followed
    these commands would be distinct from the pagan kings of
    neighboring nations; he would be faithful and, like a shep-
    herd, would guide God's people to righteous living. King
    Solomon was the wisest king the world has ever known, but
    consider carefully how he measured up in terms of obedi-
    ence to God's commands.

God's Commands	Solomon's Choices
Deut. 17:16	2 Chron. 9:25, 28
Deut. 17:17a	1 Kings 11:1 – 3
Deut. 17:17b	2 Chron. 9:13 – 14, 27

In what ways had Solomon allowed the world's culture to
shape him? How do you think this affected his ability to use
the magnificent gifts God had given him to influence the
world for God?

Reflection

Faithfulness to God can produce blessings for generations after we
are gone; disobedience can too. Just as was true for the kings of
Israel, the choices we make matter— whether to obey God and fulfill

his plans and purposes *or* to follow our own desires. May the examples of Saul and Solomon remind us why God calls us to himself and how important it is to stay true to our calling.

> When we recognize God's calling, yet fail to live it out faithfully through his power, what happens?

> Why are even our "small" acts of disobedience significant?

> How might they affect our influence and impact God's plans?

Can you think of a time when God gave (or is now giving) you an opportunity to act for him ... and you failed to do it? What have been the consequences?

Think of some examples of people in history or in your own family who lived for God. How has their obedience affected your life or influenced you?

Years after you are in heaven, how might God reward your faithfulness in the lives of people you have never known?

Day Four | A King Greater Than Solomon

The Very Words of God

> *For the grace of God that brings salvation has appeared to all men. It teaches us to say "No" to ungodliness and worldly passions, and to live self-controlled, upright and godly lives in this present age, while we wait for the blessed hope — the glorious appearing of our great God and Savior, Jesus Christ.*

> *Titus 2:11 – 13*

Bible Discovery

Committed to Fulfilling the Will of God

Solomon was the wisest king who ever lived, yet in many ways he failed to obey God. But God has sent another king, a king of his own choosing, a king who described himself as "one greater than Solomon."

1. Who is the king who is greater than Solomon? (See Matthew 12:22 – 23, 42.)

2. Jesus came to obey God and accomplish his will in all things (Luke 22:42). Read the following Scripture passages and take careful note of how Jesus viewed and went about fulfilling his purpose:

   John 4:34; 14:8 – 13

   Matthew 20:28

   Luke 4:42 – 44

Luke 19:10

John 10:7 – 11

John 18:37

3. In what ways do Jesus' purposes and values stand in contrast to the purposes and values of the world's culture?

How does living out Jesus' purposes and values help reveal God to those who do not know him?

As you consider the purposes and values Solomon lived out toward the end of his life, in what ways would you say that Jesus is greater than Solomon?

4. According to 2 Corinthians 5:20 – 21, what is to be our primary calling as Christians?

How do we fulfill that calling? (See Deuteronomy 6:5; 1 John 2:3 – 6.)

Reflection

We each have a choice to make: to follow the example of a king the world would choose or to follow the example of a king chosen by God. Our choice may make a difference not only for us in our lifetime, but for generations to come.

Take a few minutes to consider the risks and consequences of living according to the example (or "culture") of Jesus or the culture of the world.

What do you stand to gain? What do you stand to lose?

In what ways do your daily choices in response to God's calling influence your impact for God today and in the future?

In what way(s) have you allowed your culture to shape your life choices rather than allowing God to shape those choices for his purposes and his glory?

How committed are you *really* to being an ambassador for Christ and fulfilling God's will? In practical terms, what does that look like in your life?

What kinds of things could happen in our culture if more Christians took seriously their call to choose God's ways rather than the ways of the world and lived as obedient ambassadors of Christ?

Memorize

Don't you know that friendship with the world is hatred toward God? Anyone who chooses to be a friend of the world becomes an enemy of God.

James 4:4

Day Five | Assured of Victory

The Very Words of God

But thanks be to God! He gives us the victory through our Lord Jesus Christ.

1 Corinthians 15:57

Bible Discovery

We Fight the Battle, but the Victory Is Already Won

Ever since he tempted Adam and Eve to sin, Satan and his spiritual forces have done everything possible to hinder God's redemptive work on earth. Even so, Jesus, the promised Messiah, carried out God the Father's will and paid the price of redemption for all of humankind. Consider the ultimate victory the Messiah accomplished and the hope it gives as we continue to fight the battle against evil so that all the world will know the one true God.

1. What has Jesus done for us? See:

   John 3:16

Romans 5:6 – 11, 18 – 19

Galatians 1:3 – 4

1 Peter 2:24 – 25

2. Although God's creation on earth remains under Satan's influence for the present time, who has already won the victory? (See 1 John 3:8.)

    What can we be sure will happen to Satan and his evil forces? (See Matthew 25:41; 1 Corinthians 15:21 – 26.)

3. Because of what the Messiah has accomplished, what protection do we have, what weapons can we use, and what hope can we cling to as we stand firm in the fight against evil?

Scripture Text	Our Protection/Our Weapons/Our Hope
Deut. 31:6	
2 Chron. 16:9	
Ps. 18:2	
Ps. 27:5	
Ps. 34:7	

Ps. 68:35	
John 16:33	
Rom. 8:35–39	
2 Cor. 10:4	
Eph. 6:11–17	
James 4:7	
1 John 5:3–5, 11–13	
Rev. 21:2–4	

Reflection

Throughout the ages God has called his people to faithfully serve him. He has equipped us to accomplish an important task (or tasks) that will help the world know that he is God. But sometimes we have to battle the enemy who wants to distract or discourage us from accomplishing what God has given us to do.

When you face difficult battles in life, how can you experience victory?

Does "victory" mean you won't face serious challenges or experience great hardships? Why or why not?

What hope do we have, as Christians, in resisting Satan and fighting the battle against evil in our culture?

What difference does Christ's victory over Satan make in this battle?

As you seek to influence your culture and accomplish God's work, what do you receive in terms of strength, protection, and hope because of your personal relationship with Jesus?

Reread Ephesians 6:11 – 17 and practice "putting on" each piece of this "armor" until it becomes as comfortable to you in the battles you face as David's sling was to him.

Memorize

I have told you these things, so that in me you may have peace. In this world you will have trouble. But take heart! I have overcome the world.

John 16:33

We value your thoughts about what you've just read.
Please email us at *zauthor@zondervan.com*.

BIBLIOGRAPHY

History

Connolly, Peter. *Living in the Time of Jesus of Nazareth.* Tel Aviv: Steimatzky, 1983.

Ward, Kaari. *Jesus and His Times.* New York: Reader's Digest, 1987.

Whiston, William, trans. *The Works of Josephus: Complete and Unabridged.* Peabody Mass.: Hendrickson Publishers, 1987.

Wood, Leon. Revised by David O'Brien. *A Survey of Israel's History.* Grand Rapids, Mich.: Zondervan, 1986.

Jewish Roots of Christianity

Stern, David H. *Jewish New Testament Commentary.* Clarksville, Md.: Jewish New Testament Publications, 1992.

Wilson, Marvin R. *Our Father Abraham: Jewish Roots of the Christian Faith.* Grand Rapids, Mich.: Eerdmans, 1986.

Young, Brad H. *Jesus the Jewish Theologian.* Peabody, Mass.: Hendrickson Publishers, 1995.

Geography

Beitzel, Barry J. *The Moody Atlas of Bible Lands.* Chicago: Moody Press, 1993.

Gardner, Joseph L. *Reader's Digest Atlas of the Bible.* New York: Reader's Digest, 1993.

General Background

Alexander, David, and Pat Alexander, eds. *Eerdman's Handbook to the Bible.* Grand Rapids, Mich.: Eerdmans, 1983.

Butler, Trent C., ed. *Holman Bible Dictionary.* Nashville: Holman Bible Publishers, 1991.

Edersheim, Alfred. *The Life and Times of Jesus the Messiah.* Peabody, Mass.: Hendrickson Publishers, 1994.

Archaeological Background

Charlesworth, James H. *Jesus within Judaism: New Light from Exciting Archaeological Discoveries.* New York: Doubleday, 1988.

Finegan, Jack. *The Archaeology of the New Testament: The Life of Jesus and the Beginning of the Early Church.* Princeton, N.J.: Princeton University Press, 1978.

Mazar, Amihai. *Archaeology of the Land of the Bible: 10,000 – 586 BCE.* New York: Doubleday, 1990.

To learn more about the specific backgrounds of this DVD series, consult the following resources:

Avigad, Nahman. "Jerusalem in Flames — The Burnt House Captures a Moment in Time." *Biblical Archaeology Review* (November – December 1983).

Barkey, Gabriel. "The Garden Tomb — Was Jesus Buried Here?" *Biblical Archaelogy Review* (March – April 1986).

Ben Dov, Meir. "Herod's Mighty Temple Mount." *Biblical Archaelogy Review* (November – December 1986).

Bivin, David. "The Miraculous Catch." *Jerusalem Perspective* (March – April 1992).

Burrell, Barbara, Kathryn Gleason, and Ehud Netzer. "Uncovering Herod's Seaside Palace." *Biblical Archaeology Review* (May – June 1993).

Edersheim, Alfred. *The Temple.* London: James Clarke & Co., 1959.

Edwards, William D., Wesley J. Gabel, and Floyd E. Hosmer. "On the Physical Death of Jesus Christ." *Journal of American Medical Association (JAMA)* (March 21, 1986).

Flusser, David. "To Bury Caiaphas, Not to Praise Him." *Jerusalem Perspective* (July – October 1991).

Greenhut, Zvi. "Burial Cave of the Caiaphas Family." *Biblical Archaeology Review* (September – October 1992).

Hareuveni, Nogah. *Nature in Our Biblical Heritage.* Kiryat Ono, Israel: Neot Kedumim, Ltd., 1980.

Hepper, F. Nigel. *Baker Encyclopedia of Bible Plants: Flowers and Trees, Fruits and Vegetables, Ecology.* Ed. by J. Gordon Melton. Grand Rapids, Mich.: Baker, 1993.

"The 'High Priest' of the Jewish Quarter." *Biblical Archaeology Review* (May – June 1992).

Hirschfeld, Yizhar, and Giora Solar. "Sumptuous Roman Baths Uncovered Near Sea of Galilee." *Biblical Archaelogy Review* (November – December 1984).

Hohlfelder, Robert L. "Caesarea Martima: Herod the Great's City on the Sea." *National Geographic* (February 1987).

Holum, Kenneth G. *King Herod's Dream: Caesarea on the Sea.* New York: W. W. Norton, 1988.

Mazar, Benjamin. "Excavations Near Temple Mount Reveal Splendors of Herodian Jersualem." *Biblical Archaeology Review* (July – August 1980).

Nun, Mendel. *Ancient Stone Anchors and Net Sinkers from the Sea of Galilee.* Israel: Kibbutz Ein Gev, 1993. (Also available from *Jerusalem Perspective*.)

_____. "Fish, Storms, and a Boat." *Jerusalem Perspective* (March – April 1990).

_____. "The Kingdom of Heaven Is Like a Seine." *Jerusalem Perspective* (November – December 1989).

_____. "Net upon the Waters: Fish and Fishermen in Jesus' Time." *Biblical Archaeology Review* (November – December 1993).

_____. *The Sea of Galilee and Its Fishermen in the New Testament.* Israel: Kibbutz Ein Gev, 1993. (Also available from *Jerusalem Perspective*.)

Pileggi, David. "A Life on the Kinneret." *Jerusalem Perspective* (November – December 1989).

Pixner, Bargil. *With Jesus Through Galilee According to the Fifth Gospel.* Rosh Pina, Israel: Corazin Publishing, 1992.

Pope, Marvin H. "Hosanna: What It Really Means." *Bible Review* (April 1988).

Riech, Ronny. "Ossuary Inscriptions from the Caiaphas Tomb." *Jerusalem Perspective* (July – October 1991).

_____. "Six Stone Water Jars." *Jerusalem Perspective* (July – September 1995).

Ritmyer, Kathleen. "A Pilgrim's Journey." *Biblical Archaeology Review* (November – December 1989).

Ritmyer, Kathleen, and Leen Ritmyer. "Reconstructing Herod's Temple Mount in Jerusalem." *Biblical Archaeology Review* (November – December 1989).

_____. "Reconstructing the Triple Gate." *Biblical Archaeology Review* (November – December 1989).

More Great Resources
from Focus on the Family®

Volume 1: Promised Land

This volume focuses on the Old Testament — particularly on the nation of ancient Israel, God's purposes for His people and why He placed them in the Promised Land.

Volume 2: Prophets & Kings

This volume looks into the life of Israel during Old Testament times to understand how the people struggled with the call of God to be a separate and holy nation.

Volume 3: Life and Ministry of the Messiah

This volume explores the life and teaching ministry of Jesus. Discover new insights about the greatest man who ever lived.

Volume 4: Death and Resurrection of the Messiah

Witness the passion of the Messiah as He resolutely sets His face toward Jerusalem to suffer and die for His bride. Discover the thrill the disciples felt when they learned of His resurrection and were later filled with the Holy Spirit.

Volume 5: Early Church

Capture the fire of the early church with the faith lessons on Volume 5. See how the first Christians lived out their faith with a passion that literally changed the world.

Volume 6: In the Dust of the Rabbi

"Follow a rabbi, drink in his words and be covered with the dust of his feet," says the ancient Jewish proverb. Come discover how to follow Jesus as you walk with teacher and historian Ray Vander Laan through the breathtaking terrain of Israel and Turkey and explore what it really means to be a disciple.

FOR MORE INFORMATION

 Online:
Log on to www.focusonthefamily.com
In Canada, log on to www.focusonthefamily.ca.

 Phone:
Call toll free: (800) A-FAMILY
In Canada, call toll free: (800) 661-9800.

BD08XTTWMK

More Great Resources
from Focus on the Family®

Volume 7: Walk as Jesus Walked — Making Disciples

The latest in-depth study once again takes viewers to Israel, where 12 disciples walked the walk their rabbi Jesus taught them. Examining the culture and politics of the first century, Ray Vander Laan opens up the Gospels as never before.

The True Easter Story: The Promise Kept

Biblical historian Ray Vander Laan re-examines the dramatic events of Easter in The True Easter Story: The Promise Kept. New footage filmed in Israel, combined with earlier lessons from the series, show the death and resurrection of Jesus as a fulfillment of the promise God made to Abraham. Approximately 44 minutes; includes a bonus faith lesson, "Lamb of God."

The True Christmas Story: Herod the Great, Jesus the King

Experience The True Christmas Story: Herod the Great, Jesus the King, filmed in Israel with expanded footage at the site of Herod's fortress. Biblical scholar Ray Vander Laan uses earlier lessons from the series to contrast the lives of Jesus and Herod, making the Christmas story even more meaningful. This 43-minute teaching includes a bonus faith lesson, "Living Water."

FOR MORE INFORMATION

Online:
Log on to www.focusonthefamily.com
In Canada, log on to www.focusonthefamily.ca.

Phone:
Call toll free: (800) A-FAMILY
In Canada, call toll free: (800) 661-9800.

BD08XTTWMK

Share Your Thoughts

With the Author: Your comments will be forwarded to the author when you send them to *zauthor@zondervan.com*.

With Zondervan: Submit your review of this book by writing to *zreview@zondervan.com*.

Free Online Resources at
www.zondervan.com

Zondervan AuthorTracker: Be notified whenever your favorite authors publish new books, go on tour, or post an update about what's happening in their lives at www.zondervan.com/authortracker.

Daily Bible Verses and Devotions: Enrich your life with daily Bible verses or devotions that help you start every morning focused on God. Visit www.zondervan.com/newsletters.

Free Email Publications: Sign up for newsletters on Christian living, academic resources, church ministry, fiction, children's resources, and more. Visit www.zondervan.com/newsletters.

Zondervan Bible Search: Find and compare Bible passages in a variety of translations at www.zondervanbiblesearch.com.

Other Benefits: Register yourself to receive online benefits like coupons and special offers, or to participate in research.

ZONDERVAN

ZONDERVAN.com/
AUTHORTRACKER
follow your favorite authors